FRANZ KAFKA

Franz Kafka

The Poet of Shame and Guilt

SAUL FRIEDLÄNDER

Yale

UNIVERSITY

PRESS

New Haven and London

Published with assistance from the Louis Stern Memorial Fund.

To Orna

Berlin–Charlottenburg, April 10, 1917

Dear Sir,

You made me unhappy.

I bought your "Metamorphosis" as a gift for my cousin. But, she is incapable of understanding the story. My cousin gave it to her mother who doesn't understand it either. The mother gave the book to my other cousin, who also didn't find an explanation. Now they have written to me: They expect me to explain the story to them as I am the doctor in the family. But I am at a loss.

Sir! I have spent months in the trenches exchanging blows with the Russians without batting an eyelid. But I could not stand losing my good name with my cousins. Only you can help me. You must do it, as you are the one who landed me in this mess. So please tell me what my cousin should think about "Metamorphosis."

Most respectfully yours,
Dr. Siegfried Wolff

CONTENTS

ACKNOWLEDGMENTS

WRITING THIS BOOK has been a rather solitary experience in scholarly terms, as I am not closely acquainted with Kafka specialists, or with specialists in German literature, critical theory, and the like. I feel grateful nonetheless to quite a number of scholars in these domains whose work has helped me along: they are repeatedly mentioned throughout the text.

There is one exception, however, to this quasi-anonymity: the reader of the manuscript for Yale University Press (who agreed to share his name with me), Mark M. Anderson from Columbia University; Anderson was so generous in his comments and so attentive in his suggestions and corrections that I owe him very special thanks.

Apart from scholarly advice, I am greatly indebted to a few people for their confidence and help. To Georges Borchardt, my agent, who suggested my name to Yale University Press for the Kafka volume in the Jewish Lives series; to Ileene Smith and John Palmer, the editorial director and managing editor of the series, for their constant assistance and advice; to John Donatich, the director of the Press, for helping me out in dealing with the staggering demands submitted by the publisher owning the rights to Kafka's translations. My thanks are also addressed to Dan Heaton, my excellent copyeditor.

Much closer to home, I immensely benefited from Amir Kenan's word-processing wizardry and from his outstanding editorial skills. Mainly, I couldn't have written this book, with all the doubts and the uncertainty that accompanied it, without the constant support and the frequent advice of my wife, Orna, to whom it is dedicated.

———◆—◆—◆———

Introduction

IN *THE BROTHERS KARAMAZOV*, Dostoevsky evokes a painting that shows a peasant immobile in the snow, lost in contemplation. The man is not aware of any thinking; he lets impressions accumulate in him, imperceptibly, without knowing to what end. After allowing these impressions to grow over time, he will possibly leave for Jerusalem in search of salvation or burn down his native village. Maybe, he will do both . . .[1]

There is some resemblance between this moujik and Franz Kafka's "K." in *The Castle*, as he reaches the apparent end of his voyage, late on a wintry night. "The village," Kafka wrote, "lay under deep snow. There was no sign of the castle hill, fog and darkness surrounded it, not even the faintest glow of light suggested the large castle. K. stood for a long time on the wooden bridge that heads from the main road to the village, gazing upward into seeming emptiness."[2] What follows can appear as a hopeless pilgrimage to an inaccessible Jerusalem or an equally hopeless attempt to subvert the immobile life of the village and of its relations with the castle, maybe both—and maybe none of it.

We may assume from the story that K. knew of the castle and of its location before arriving and thus the "seeming" emptiness couldn't have misled him.[3] And yet, this gazing into an emptiness created by a veil of fog and darkness has something mystical about it. K. may have sensed that behind the veil, an entire world, the object of his own longings, was either welcoming or rejecting him. But didn't the obscurity as such, the absence of even a flicker of light, signify that before crossing the wooden bridge into the village, K. should have abandoned all hope? A "divine comedy" or the mere rejection of an imposter? In Kafka's world the sacred and the profane cannot be untangled, and "seeming" may be the weightiest word in his writings.

I

I had read my first book about Franz Kafka—Max Brod's biography in its French translation—during my Parisian high school days, most probably in 1947. When I arrived in Israel, in 1948, and went to stay with an uncle in a village inhabited by Czech Jews (most of whom, like my uncle, had arrived from Prague in 1939), I discovered the same biography—in its original German this time. I was told on that occasion that Brod himself had been a houseguest before moving to Tel Aviv. Upon leaving he had taken chairs that he never returned. A few months later, my uncle sent me to the agricultural boarding school Ben Shemen, first established in Berlin by Siegfried Lehmann during World War I as a home for Eastern European Jewish children (officially: Jewish People's Home); in the thirties, it was transferred to Palestine. In 1916 Kafka discussed the Home at great length with his fiancée, Felice Bauer; he encouraged her to volunteer for work with the youngsters in

Lehmann's institution. And, Kafka met Dora Diamant, his last companion, in Müritz on the Baltic Sea in 1923, when she was working at a summer camp for the Home's children and he was vacationing nearby.

My family's world was that of Prague Jews, belonging to a slightly younger cohort than Franz's generation. Theirs was a quiet middle-class existence; they were relatively well-off and considered themselves politically safe, notwithstanding ever more threatening rumblings during later years. They spoke German better than Czech (yet spoke Czech nonetheless). A few among them were interested in Zionism, but, with rare exceptions, those who emigrated to Palestine at the very last moment did so only by dint of the most catastrophic circumstances.

My father studied at the German Law School of Charles University, which Kafka had attended some fifteen years before; like Kafka, he eventually became legal adviser in a Prague insurance company. My mother's family lived in the German-speaking area of Northern Bohemia in Ober-Rochlitz (which Kafka mentions as Röchlitz, near Gablonz, which he visited several times). My mother's first name was Elli (Gabriele), as was that of Franz's eldest sister. And, like those of Kafka's three sisters, my parents' lives ended in German camps. All these hidden links, discovered over time, may have added to my predilection for Kafka's texts, beyond the appeal of their intrinsic greatness. In and of itself, however, this would not have convinced me of writing on a topic so far removed from my field, history, but for very specific and hardly mentioned issues that I considered important enough to be brought up in a small biographical essay.

"A glance at any bibliography of writings on Kafka," wrote Erich Heller, "shows how problematic it is to add to the superabundance of books and articles on him."[4] A common remark, except for the fact that Heller wrote these lines in 1974. During the thirty-eight years that have gone by since, thousands of new titles have been added. Heller elegantly shifts part of the blame onto Kafka himself: "Kafka's share of the blame lies in his being the creator of the most obscure lucidity in the history of literature, a phenomenon that, like a word one has on the tip of one's tongue, perpetually attracts and at the same time repels the search for what it is and means."[5]

This "obscure lucidity" has led indeed to the most extraordinary array of contextual and textual interpretations (and ignited confrontations as intense as in the world of historians . . .). In contextual terms, Kafka appeared as a neurotic Jew, a religious one, a mystic, a self-hating Jew, a crypto-Christian, a Gnostic, the messenger of an antipatriarchal brand of Freudianism, a Marxist, the quintessential existentialist, a prophet of totalitarianism or of the Holocaust, an iconic voice of High Modernism, and much more; in short, he has become the most protean cultural figure of the past century. And beyond such encompassing or monothematic identifications extends a scholarly jungle, often lamented, but spreading nonetheless.

Kafka was no builder of theories, no designer of systems; he followed dreams, created metaphors and unexpected associations; he told stories; he was a poet. His frequent use of religious allusions (either directly or implicitly, either Christian of Jewish) may create confusion, but such allusions are mostly laced with irony and do not indicate religious faith. Mainly, Kafka was the poet of his own disorder.

Throughout his life, Kafka struggled with some pervasive problems that left traces in his daily existence and, even more so, in his imaginary world. These problems and the issues I will discuss in the next section led to quasi-obsessive soul-searching, as documented in his *Diaries* and in his letters (and, indirectly, in his fiction). Thus, at first glance, there is nothing astonishing in the penultimate entry of his *Diaries*, on December 18, 1922 (the last entry was written a few months later, on June 12, 1923). Kafka, thoroughly aware of his fast-declining health, noted: "All this time in bed. Yesterday *Either/Or.*"[6] Nonetheless, this entry is perplexing on several counts. Søren Kierkegaard's *Either/Or* is an examination of two opposed ways of living: the esthetic life and the moral one. According to a letter to Max Brod of January 20, 1918, Kafka started reading the book in those days.[7] He didn't like the first volume (the esthetic life), which included "The Diary of a Seducer," and in mid-March 1918 he wrote to Brod: "I still cannot read the first book of *Either/Or* without repugnance."[8] Yet almost five years later, as he was getting increasingly weaker, Kafka was reading *Either/Or* once again.

We have no indication about the way Kafka reacted to this further reading, but couldn't it be that this renewed pondering of Kierkegaard's dichotomy resulted from some unresolved moral issue that weighed on Kafka throughout the years?

Treasures of erudition have been spent on recording the tiniest details of Kafka's life and on excavating the philological, literary, and philosophical foundations of each of his metaphors or name games. Yet although the discovery of any glistening pebble may have been considered a signpost to a gold mine, some huge spires towering over Kafka territory—his sense of shame and guilt, perceived by every reader—have elicited mainly very general and abstract interpretations that do not sufficiently point to the personal anguish from which they stemmed.

"Franz Kafka," wrote George Steiner, "lived original sin. . . . A mere handful of individuals have endured in their daily existence the conviction and consequence of their fallen state. Like Pascal and Søren Kierkegaard, . . . Kafka knew hours, days perhaps, in which he identified personal life itself with indescribable existential guilt. To be alive, engender further life, was to sin."[9]

Kafka's sense of shame didn't fare better. "Seventy years

after his death," John Updike wrote in his 1995 foreword to *The Complete Stories*, "Kafka epitomizes one aspect of [the] modern mind-set: a sensation of anxiety and shame whose center cannot be located and therefore cannot be placated."[10] A sensation of shame as an aspect of the modern mind-set?

If, however, you are an "imposter," like K. in *The Castle*, pretending to be what you are not, showing a mask to the world in order to hide your true face, then you may feel shame or even guilt. K. didn't feel shame or guilt as he had convinced himself, before trying to convince others, that he indeed was and had been a "land surveyor."[11] K. was a master in self-deception, but Kafka was not. What, then, could have been the issue that sufficiently weighed on him to lead to this rereading of *Either/Or?*

2

The immediate sources for this query are Kafka's personal writings (the *Diaries* and the *Letters*); the "findings" will reappear in many disguises in the fiction, as we shall later see. Regarding the immediate sources, Max Brod turns out to be an unexpected guide. The "friend" made it his aim to turn Kafka into a "saint." In his 1937 biography, he was quite explicit about Kafka's "saintliness," provoking the anger of Walter Benjamin, among others, but, nonetheless, leading an entire generation of commentators astray. To bolster his arguments, Brod may have hidden or eliminated part of the correspondence between young Franz and his intimate friend Oskar Pollak, possibly out of his own dislike for Pollak and his envy of the close relation between the two young men. He declared later that those letters were destroyed during the war.[12] Then, as he acquired the diaries and the most important parts of Kafka's correspondence, he systematically censored whatever seemed to him to threaten his friend's saintly image (although he missed a few hints in the *Diaries* that later were deleted in the English translation, probably with his assent). As a result of his intervention, Brod became a "guide," *malgré lui*, once the full critical edition of Kafka's writings was published in the late 1980s and early 1990s, on the basis of the original manuscripts. It sufficed to compare Brod's edition with the new critical edition to discover what Brod had attempted to hide, the more so that he certainly understood Franz's allusions and made sure to leave them unpublished in his own version of the writings.[13]

These *Diaries* and the *Letters* indicate clearly enough that — except for the constant pondering about his writing, the quintessence of his being — the issues torturing Kafka most of his life were of a sexual nature. So far, nobody would disagree: Kafka feared sexual intercourse with his female friends, was apparently disgusted by it, saw it as a punishment (in his own words); some commentators mention impotence; Jacques Derrida, in his reading of "Before the Door of the Law," explicitly used, in a Freudian sense, the association to *ante portas* ("before the door"), that is, premature ejaculation.[14] Yet therein we could be accessing the domain of *shame*, but unlikely that of guilt.

It is Kafka himself who prods us on. On August 26, 1920, he wrote to a female friend, the Czech journalist Milena Jesenska, possibly his closest confidant: "I am dirty, Milena, infinitely dirty, this is why I scream so much about purity. No one sings as purely as those who inhabit the deepest hell—what we take to be the song of angels is their song."[15] Something tormented Kafka, but he did not say more. All the sources indicate, however, that his feelings of guilt were related not to some concrete initiatives on his part but to fantasies, to *imagined sexual possibilities*.

Quite a few interpreters have occasionally alluded to homoerotic urges in Kafka's life; but Mark Anderson seems to be the only one who has gone beyond sporadic allusions and considered homoeroticism as central to Kafka's life and work.[16]

Kafka himself didn't make things easy. Nowhere did he explicitly admit that he harbored homosexual tendencies. Throughout, Kafka pretended interest in women, courted women, commented on women, visited brothels, and the like. And yet, as we shall see, indirect allusions (but no admissions) to other urges abound in his diaries, his letters, and his fiction.

The move from the personal domain to the fictional one is of course what imports here (beyond pointing to potential sources of shame and guilt feelings). Before turning to that crucial mutation, however, let me add a few remarks regarding the personal level. Even if we take into account Kafka's petit bourgeois environment, the restricted world and norms of the Jewish Prague middle class during the first three decades of the twentieth century, it is hard to believe that Franz internalized the surrounding norms to the point of considering his homoerotic leanings as "dirty." What he alluded to, we do not know. Perhaps he opaquely refers to his sexual attraction to adolescents, even children? But these, like his homoerotic urges more generally, remained in the domain of fantasy. Could he have felt "dirty" because of fantasies? Hadn't he read or heard of *Death in Venice*, for example, or of Stefan George's "Maximin"? The interpretation of Mann's stories may have remained traditional before the publication of his *Diaries*, and perhaps Kafka didn't understand the German novelist's camouflage; regarding George, no such problem existed.[17] But whatever the case may be on the personal level, it is indeed its impact on Kafka's writings that is of the essence. In some important cases, there is an almost direct transposition from one level to the other. Here, one example should suffice.

At the end of January 1922, Kafka arrived at Hotel Krone in Spindelmühle, a mountain resort in northeast Bohemia, and almost immediately started working on *The Castle*. A few days later, in his diary entry of February 2 (the words censored in the English translation but left by Brod in the German one are in square brackets), he noted: "Struggle on the road to [the] Tannenstein in the morning, struggle while watching the ski-jumping contest. Happy little B., in all his innocence somehow shadowed by my ghosts, at least in my eyes [, specially his outstretched leg in its gray rolled-up sock], his aimless wandering glance, his aimless talk. In this connection it occurs to me—but this is already forced—that towards evening he wanted to go home with me."[18]

Happy and innocent little B. reappears in *The Castle* as Hans B[runswick], the young boy who, on his own initiative, knocks at K.'s door, in the schoolroom where K. lives with Frieda, to help him and be his ally against the hostile surroundings. Little B. is lovingly described, but in most (maybe all) interpretations of *The Castle*, the episode remains disconnected from the exegesis of this particularly enigmatic and the last of Kafka's three novels.

Strongly fought (but not repressed—that is, not unconscious) homoerotic urges—and possibly even more haunting sexual fantasies—not only were present throughout Franz Kafka's life, but they seem to have had an impact on diverse other personal issues, whether he fully recognized it or not. Let me stress this point in order to avoid any misunderstanding, particularly any reductive interpretation of Kafka's anguished self-perception. Thus, for example, Kafka's doubts about his own body were probably enhanced and twisted by the antisemitic tags about the feminization of the Jewish body (and personality), common in Central Europe at the turn of the century, as we shall see. In other words, self-perception and elements of the cultural environment may have merged in a toxic synthesis that became part and parcel of Kafka's complicated relation to his Jewish identity.[19]

Let us briefly turn back to the essential, to the relation between Kafka's general feelings of shame and guilt, his specific self-accusations ("I am dirty, Milena . . ."), and his fictional world. Not much (except in a case like that of "little B.") seems at first to allow for a simple transposition; the mutation from the "real" to the symbolic level may have followed any number of paths. Yet, more often than expected, the text appears to point to both worlds at one and the same time, as if, in repeated instances, Kafka's fiction was but a more or less heavily disguised autobiography. Could it not be one of the ways of interpreting Joseph K.'s last thought in the last sentence of *The Trial*? "'Like a Dog!' he said; it was as if the shame of it must outlive him." And couldn't the same autobiographical dimension help in understanding why in Kafka's world nobody is considered and treated as innocent, even those who look the most innocent: "Rossman and K., the innocent and the guilty [Rossman is the main character of *Amerika*, K. of *The Trial*]," Kafka noted in his *Diary* on September 30, 1915, "both executed without distinction in the end, the guilty one [should read 'the innocent one'] with a gentler hand, more pushed aside than struck down." [20] Indeed, many—possibly most—of Kafka's characters commit suicide, are executed, thrown out as trash, lost forever in the wilderness, or otherwise destroyed by others or by themselves. In Kafka's world, there is no redemption. What looks like redemption becomes the target of his implacable irony.

Thus the specific mutations of Kafka's shame and guilt and, at times, of his sexual urges as such may appear in the fiction in hardly camouflaged form or else under the most unexpected masks. Some of these transpositions will be analyzed in the coming chapters; they appear both in the short stories and in the three novels, often in relation to central figures: women. Kafka's representation of women is grimacing at best. And as these feminine characters are at the core of the three novels, the entire structure and unfolding of their narratives comes to depend upon this element.

3

Although the personal dimension was crucial in essential parts of Kafka's fiction, this biographical essay nonetheless aims at integrating it in a wider synthesis. This demands a somewhat independent account of Kafka's relations with his family, his attitude to his Jewish identity, the political, social, intellectual, and mainly literary influences on his writings, and these writings as such, as the mold of new worlds and as weapons in Kafka's struggle against the world. In great part, I will rely on the vast existing scholarship in these diverse domains, but I shall also try my hand at interpretations of texts that differ from interpretations already available (the reader may take this with a skeptical smile or, possibly, with a frown). Two guiding theses should allow me to structure these multiple arguments: first, Kafka's ongoing ambivalence between adaptation and rebellion and, second, the major line of defense used in his texts: irony.

Very early on Kafka must have felt that he was *different* from most of those who surrounded him, different in his erotic cravings and different in the powers of imagination and expression he sensed within himself. Externally, he adapted: to the family surroundings that he left for good less than a year before dying; to the externals of dating and pretending he wished to marry; to steady rise as an exemplary official in a state insurance company. These were all facets of an adaptation he hated to various degrees. And while he acted his part in the world, he defended himself by fiercely subverting that same world in his writings. In his fiction he demolished the very norms to which he submitted in his everyday life: Authority, Justice, the Rule of Law, the very logic of human communication. Franz Kafka: the anarcho-conformist . . .

I shall try to follow the interplay between adaptation and rebellion in the main domains of Kafka's life by turning, each time, both to the external circumstances of his existence and to those sequences in the fiction that amplify, transform, and yet probe the depths of the apparently simple unfolding of everyday existence.

Kafka's last diary entry, on June 12, 1923, dealt with the psychological torture produced by the fast progressing illness; and then: "The only consolation would be: it happens whether you like it or not. And what you like is of infinitesimally little help. More than consolation is: You too have weapons."[21] The weapons were writing as such, of course, and, by way of it, the unleashing of Kafka's fierce irony.

What is meant here by "writing as such" is the process that anybody who ever read a few pages of Kafka's fiction will immediately recognize: the appearances of the "real world" are kept, but, like in a dream, its substance is inexorably dissolved until the cardboard reality ultimately collapses. Kafka's method of de-realization has been studied by many of his interpreters; I found no better way of describing it than by reversing the characterization that biographer Richard Ellmann applied to James Joyce's world: "Joyce's discovery," wrote Ellmann, "was that the ordinary is the extraordinary."[22] Kafka's discovery was that the extraordinary is the ordinary.

Let me add a few words about Kafka's irony. Thomas Mann has been dubbed "The Ironic German."[23] How should Kafka be labeled? The ironic Jew? There were "ironic Jews" in Kafka's times: Kurt Tucholsky, Maximilian Harden, and mainly Karl Kraus (all of them converted Jews). They were "professional" ironists; Kafka doesn't belong among them: his irony wasn't social, political, or cultural. It was either deeply personal, directed at himself, or, literally, metaphysical, like that strongest of lights he evokes in his aphorisms, meant to disintegrate the last particle of certainty, the last grain of "Truth." Some of Kafka's irony appears as an extension of his humor, of his appe-

tite for laughing, for pranks; most of it sounds as a cry of de-
fiance, like Don Giovanni's rejection of repentance while the
Commendatore is dragging him to hell.

But it isn't always easy to determine where, in which category, this irony belongs. Often, the text looks playful and "soft,"
but is it really? Thus, on October 19, 1921, Kafka noted in his
diary: "Moses fails to enter Canaan not because his life is too
short but because it is a human life. This ending of the Pentateuch bears a resemblance to the final scene of *L'Éducation sen-
timentale.*"[24] The final scene of Flaubert's *L'Éducation?* Frederic
Moreau and his closest friend Deslauriers were back in their
childhood town, Nogent, from the heady years spent in Paris,
where they had arrived with high expectations and from which
they had returned after losing all their illusions. They reminisced about their adolescence in Nogent and recalled that un-
forgettable moment when both absconded from school to the
local brothel; hardly had they come in before both ran away.
They now told each other the story, reminding one another
of every detail. "'This is the best we had!' said Frederic. 'Yes,
maybe! This is the best we had!' said Deslauriers." Thus ends
the novel—like the ending of the Pentateuch?

But all irony set aside, how, out of so many contradictions,
out of so much ambivalence, could Kafka create not a coherent self but a coherent imaginary construct to fight his most
secret struggles, to defend himself against his most intimate
demons and against the "real world" as such? Although we
can but very tentatively follow the mutations of Kafka's frag-
mented life into some of the building blocks of his fiction, we
can travel part of the road and, like in Kafka's story, locate seg-
ments of "the great wall of China," the planned defense against
the "barbarians from the North." We will never know what
message the dying Emperor sent to the builders and confided
to an envoy who lost his way. But, we can try to guess; wasn't

it possibly: "Give up hope. You will never complete that great wall"?

A brief summing up about the structure of the essay may be helpful at this point. In the first part, I mainly pursue the themes of shame and guilt, in Kafka's rendition of family relations, his reactions to perceptions of the Jewish body and, more generally, of his fellow Jews' deficiencies. In the second part, although keeping to these central issues in each of the three chapters, I widen the scope to include the other major (and related) themes: Kafka's adaptation to an existence he hated and thoroughly subverted in his writings, his bitter irony throughout, his selective relation to his cultural environment, the ongoing and increasingly desperate search for a resolution of the most intimate obsessions in some higher level of meaning, and its ultimate failure.

Part I

"Prague Doesn't Let Go . . ."

I

The Son

KAFKA LEFT HIS FAMILY home barely a few months before his death from tuberculosis in June 1924, at age forty-one. And, symbolically, even this separation did not last long: in Prague's new Jewish cemetery, Franz, his father, Hermann, and his mother, Julie, are buried under the same tombstone. At the base of the stone, a plaque commemorates Franz's three sisters, Elli, Valli, and Ottla. And yet . . .

"In the family," Franz wrote to Elli in 1921, regarding the education of her son Felix, "clutched in the tight embrace of the parents, there is room only for certain kinds of people who conform to certain kinds of requirements. . . . If they do not conform, they are not expelled—that would be very fine, but is impossible, for we are dealing with an organism here—but accursed or consumed or both."[1]

The image of the family as an organism appears in *The Metamorphosis*, Kafka's best-known story. There, however, it becomes an organism to which the son, Gregor Samsa, suddenly transformed into a huge bug, is fatally attached but also one that rejects him, more grievously each time. According to Stéphane Moses's interpretation, Kafka's story takes place in three concentric spaces: the most peripheral one is the outside world (beyond the family apartment) to which all non-family members successively flee, from Gregor's office manager to the last of the maids. The real drama plays itself out in the two spaces belonging to the family: the living room and Gregor's room. Three times, in the three parts of the story, Gregor attempts to join his family in crawling out of his room into the living room, and three times he is chased back, at first only slightly wounded, then hit by the fatal apple thrown by his father, and finally forced back, never to emerge again until his remains are thrown away as trash.[2] For Gregor, the son who still feels human, who carries a human soul within a monstrous body but has lost the ability to communicate, the most basic emotional need impels him to join the family, but the family severs the umbilical cord and lets him die; no, it hounds him to death. In fiction.

In the outside world, Franz Kafka adapted; in the family space, tension sporadically erupted; in his private space, Franz wove the complex tapestry of fantastic fathers and no less fantastic sons.

I

Prague was the outside world. A few years before World War I, the Jews of the city made up about six percent of a population of 440,000 inhabitants, Czech in the immense majority but politically dominated by a minority of Germans who, in Bohemia, within the Austro-Hungarian Empire, were becoming increasingly nationalist in the face of growing Czech nationalism. The Jews, mostly middle class, were still linguistically and culturally closer to the Germans than to the Czechs, but equally disliked by both groups: the Germans considered them interlopers, and most Czechs perceived them as supporters of Germanic domination.

From the 1860s to the 1890s, Emperor Franz Joseph's benevolent rule was supported by a liberal wave in politics. In the 1890s extremist mass movements with core antisemitic messages grew rapidly and influenced the political atmosphere throughout the Dual Monarchy. Thus, during the last years of the century, German anti-Czech riots took on an additional anti-Jewish dimension; almost immediately thereafter, Czech anti-German violence evolved in the same way, and, finally, a full-fledged Czech ritual murder accusation (the Hilsner affair) hit the Jews of Bohemia, particularly in the province, and further exacerbated antisemitism for several years. Nonetheless, at the beginning of the twentieth century and throughout World War I, anti-Jewish agitation subsided for the most part in Prague: the Jews of the city enjoyed a period of calm and—except for the war years—growing prosperity.[3]

For Franz, the child and the adolescent, outside world and family space were one. Born on July 3, 1883, he was the first of six children: the two brothers who followed, Georg and Heinrich, died in infancy; then, three sisters, Elli, Valli, and Ottla, arrived. Except for a short period, in 1912, Franz remained very close to Ottla throughout his life.

His mother, Julie Löwy, came from a relatively well-to-do background, still pious in her parents' generation but with thoroughly assimilated and successful brothers active in various parts of the world—including Franz's favorite uncle, Siegfried, a country doctor in Triesch (Moravia). His father, Hermann, came from a much poorer family, as the son of a butcher in Wossek, in the Czech province. After a difficult childhood, then several years in the army, Hermann tried his hand at a number of small ventures until, at age thirty, he met and married Julie. The dowry allowed him to launch a haberdashery that was to expand considerably over the years. Throughout, Hermann's business and the Kafkas' apartment were either at the same address or very close by, near the Altstädter Ring, the heart of the Old Town—on the outskirts of the former ghetto.

At age ten, Franz moved from the elementary school on Fleischmarkt Street to the German Gymnasium in the Kinsky-Palais, a few steps from home; two-thirds of the students were Jews. After the usual years of uninspiring rote learning, marred by Franz's complete inability to master mathematics, passing the final exam (Abitur), in May 1901, meant entering the outer domain of independent choices, at the university and along all paths of a young man's life. Franz decided to live at home, and in the fall of 1901, he entered the Law School of the German Charles University in his native city. At first glance, young Kafka doesn't appear as an adventurous soul.

In order to offset the dreariness of law studies, Franz added a few courses in German literature, but he dutifully kept to his main path and obtained his doctoral degree in law in 1906. A clerical position in the law office of a relative was followed by the mandatory stint as court intern. Once freed of these obligations, Franz found employment in the branch of an Italian insurance company in Prague and, soon thereafter, in the semi-governmental Workers' Accident Insurance Institute. There, steadily well remunerated, he would rise over the years to positions of major responsibility and stay until his retirement due to illness, in 1922.

The early years of Kafka's adult life do not seem to have been overburdened by material or other worries. In September 1909, while vacationing in Riva, on the Garda Lake in northern Italy, he sent a short note to his sister Ottla in Prague: "Dearest Ottla, please work diligently in the store, so that I may have a good time here without any worry, and give my greetings to our dear parents."[4]

While the earliest and very close friendship between Franz and fellow student Oskar Pollak waned during the later university years, Kafka became ever closer to Max Brod, one year his junior and his friend for life. All in all, this seems to have been a time of high spirits if Franz's letters are any indication. Thus in March 1908 he writes to Brod: "I have had an almost excellent idea which can be carried out very cheaply. Instead of our planned nightlife from Monday to Tuesday we could arrange a nice morning life, meeting at five o'clock or half past five at the Mary statue—then we won't have to let the women down—and go to the Trokadero or to Kuchelbad or to the Eldorado [the Trokadero and the Eldorado were wine cellars, Kuchelbad a racetrack outside Prague]. Then, depending on how we feel, we could have coffee in the garden by the Moldau or else leaning against Joszi's shoulders. Both possibilities have their points."[5]

To the Trokadero and the Eldorado, where Franz and his friends (by then, mainly Max Brod, Felix Weltsch, and Willy Haas) spent many a late evening, one can add the nightclubs Lucerna and London, the first film halls in Prague, several theaters, the opera and, of course, any number of cafés, where intellectuals and writers congregated: the Louvre, the Arco, and others. The Fanta circle, and its lectures and debates, will be revisited later.

In 1905 for the first time Franz arrived in a sanatorium (Zuckmantel in Austrian Silesia) for a hydrotherapy cure meant to alleviate his chronic insomnia. It is there that, according to an entry in his diary many years later, he had his first intimate relations with an older (and experienced) woman, whose identity he did not reveal.[6] Otherwise, as we shall see, the coming years would be a time of many flirtations but no full-fledged affairs until, in August 1912, he met at the Brods' a young Jewish woman from Berlin, Felice Bauer, who was to become his fiancée and with whom he would share an intense (mostly epistolary) relation—but briefly interrupted—for more than five years.

2

When, for the first time in her son's room, mother Samsa set her eyes on Gregor the bug, she fainted: "And as if giving up completely, she fell with outstretched arms across the couch and did not stir."[7] A completely distraught Gregor ventured into the living room; he was soon chased back by the furious father who started bombarding him with apples, one of which "forced its way into Gregor's back."[8] "With his last glance he saw the door of his room burst open as his mother rushed out ahead of his screaming sister, in her chemise, for his sister had partly undressed her while she lay unconscious . . . saw his mother run up to his father and on the way her unfastened petticoats slide to the floor one by one; and saw as, stumbling over the skirts she forced herself unto his father, and embracing him, in complete union with him—but now Gregor's sight went dim—her hands clasping his father's neck, begged for Gregor's life."[9]

The story points to the mother's confused attitude toward her son, and to her unquestioned dependence upon and total union with the father. Franz's own feelings for his mother were lukewarm at times—and he admitted his "occasional coldness" toward her; it seems, however, that his affection for her grew with time, although he knew that her foremost loyalty was to her husband. In his 1919 "Letter to his Father," Franz recognized his mother's inextricable dilemma, set as she was between her husband and her son:

> It is true that Mother was endlessly good to me, but for me all that was in relation to you [Father], that is to say, in no good relation. Mother unconsciously played the part of a beater during a hunt . . . by talking sensibly (in the confusion of my

childhood she was the very prototype of good sense and reasonableness), by pleading for me; and I was again driven back into your orbit, which I might perhaps otherwise have broken out of, to your advantage and to my own. Or it happened that no real reconciliation came about, that Mother merely shielded me from you in secret, secretly gave me something, and then where you were concerned, I was again the furtive creature, the cheat, the guilty one, who in his worthlessness could only pursue sneaky methods ever to get the things he regarded as his right. . . . This again meant an increase in the sense of guilt.[10]

Franz's main target was the father.

Franz wrote his "Letter to His Father" in November 1919, four and a half years before his death; in his own words, it was "a lawyer's brief" that, in fact, was never delivered to the addressee.[11] Its immediate trigger was purely haphazard—the father's opposition to Franz's engagement to Julie Wohryzek, a synagogue custodian's daughter whose social status Hermann considered unworthy of the Kafkas. Thus the letter was a sudden crystallization of arguments that the son must have rehashed and reformulated in his mind for many years.

Whether Hermann was as uncouth and boorish as Franz describes him is unlikely; but that is how, the son argues in the "Letter," he perceived and experienced him.[12] According to the letter, Franz felt humiliated and shamed by Hermann—even when the father's intention was entirely different: the trips to the public swimming pool on the Vltava (Moldau) are a case in point.

"At that time [Franz's childhood], and at that time in every way, I would have needed encouragement. I was, after all, weighed down by your mere physical presence. I remember, for instance, how we often undressed in the same bathing hut. There was I, skinny, weakly, slight; you strong, tall, broad." The comparison goes on and Franz feels increasingly humiliated as they step out of the hut, "you holding me by the hand, a little skeleton, unsteady, barefoot on the boards, frightened of the water, incapable of copying your swimming strokes, which you, with the best of intentions, but actually to my profound humiliation kept on demonstrating, then I was frantic with desperation and at such moments all my bad experiences in all areas fitted magnificently together."[13]

Franz's recollections of Hermann's humiliating behavior include the most diverse episodes, from the father's attitude toward Franz's friends, to his writing, to his renewed interest in Judaism, to his supposed lack of experience in sexual matters. Nothing is left intact and yet, throughout the "Letter," there is a strong ambivalence. Franz attacks and retreats almost immediately.

"Fortunately," he writes at some stage,

> there were exceptions to all this, mostly you suffered in silence, and affection and kindliness by their own strength overcame all obstacles, and moved me immediately. Rare as it was, it was wonderful. For instance, in earlier years, in hot summers, when you were tired after lunch, I saw you having a nap at the office, your elbow on the desk; or you joined us in the country, in the summer holidays, on Sundays, worn out from work; or the time Mother was gravely ill and you stood holding on to the bookcase, shaking with sobs; or when, during my last illness, you came tiptoeing to Ottla's room to see me, stopping in the doorway, craning your neck to see me and out of consideration only waved to me with your hand. At such times one would lie back and weep for happiness, and one weeps now, writing it down.[14]

Kafka dedicated the volume of stories *A Country Doctor* to his father; it was published in 1920. In 1918 he had commented on the dedication in a letter to Brod: "Ever since I decided to dedicate this book to my father, I am deeply concerned to have it appear soon." He then added, in a somewhat sad and wistful tone: "Not that I could appease my father this way; the roots of our antagonism are too deep, but I would at least have done something; if I haven't emigrated to Palestine, I will at any rate have traced the way there on the map."[15]

There was more. On October 1st, 1911, Kafka described the Kol Nidre service on Yom Kippur eve at the Altneu Synagogue. It is an oft-quoted text, brilliantly ironic. But it ends on a less familiar note: "I was stirred immeasurably more deeply by Judaism in the Pinkas Synagogue."[16] Hermann Kafka had been on the board of the Pinkas Synagogue; thus it was with his father that Franz attended the services that stirred him deeply.[17] It was a communion with Judaism, but wasn't it one with the father as well?

Ultimately, in a last expression of deep care for his parents, Franz wished to spare them the sight of his physical devastation, as the end was nearing. Less than two weeks before his death, on May 19, 1924, in a letter clearly directed at both of them, he avoided their visit, describing signs of impending amelioration and envisioning the possibility of spending some time together, in the not too distant future. The first paragraph gives the tone: "Dearest Parents, now about the visits you refer to every so often. I have been considering the matter every day, for it is very important to me; we have not been together peacefully in a beautiful locality, alone. I don't remember when the last time was—once for a few hours in Franzensbad. And then 'having a good glass of beer together,' as you write, from which I see that Father doesn't think much of this year's wine, and I'll agree with him there, as far as the beer is concerned. In the past, as I often remember, during the heat spells we used to have beer together quite often, in the far-off time Father would take me along to the Civilian Swimming Pool."[18]

The tense relation between Franz and his father can be seen, in part at least, as a faraway echo (but an echo nonetheless) of the generational confrontation that, by the turn of the century, pitted middle-class European youth against the "materialism" and the "hypocrisy" of the parents' bourgeois generation. This thoroughly described and interpreted confrontation surfaced under different guises, from revolutionary politics on the Left and on the Right to youth movements (the Wandervögel in Germany before World War I, the Bünde afterward), to cultural manifestations (Expressionism and the like), and, increasingly, to a radical transformation of the public sphere, the intellectual climate and the aesthetic landscape, even more rapidly so in Austria than anywhere else in Central Europe.[19]

The rebellion was particularly intense among Jewish middle-class youth, mainly in Central and part of Eastern Europe, in a world in which the parents' generation had just made it to the ranks of the bourgeoisie (without being accepted by surrounding non-Jewish society), a situation that at times led to the exacerbated need for showing off among these "parvenus," in Hannah Arendt's terms, and/or to the pseudocultural pretenses of a basically still uneducated group.

The Jewish "sons," who frequently acquired the higher education open to them, were often unable to deal with the "grossness" of the fathers or their mendacity (also in terms of religious observance), while the fathers, self-made men as they were, had no patience for what in their eyes appeared as the overindulgent lifestyles of the sons and what they considered the sheer ungratefulness of their progeny.

On occasion, indeed, Franz's complaints are literally hard to comprehend: "In the large room there was the clamor of card playing," Franz writes down in January 1912, "and later the usual conversation which Father carries on when he is well, as he is today, loudly if not coherently. . . . Little Felix [Elli's and Karl Hermann's son] slept in the girls' room, the door of which was wide open. I slept across the way, in my own room. The door of this room, in consideration of my age, was closed.

Besides, the open door indicated that they still wanted to lure Felix into the family while I was already excluded."[20]

The twenty-nine-year-old Franz, still holed up in his childhood room, is in fact competing for his parents' love and attention with two-month-old Felix, his nephew, born on December 8, 1911. Incidentally, the door to Felix's room was probably left open in order to hear him crying; it is unlikely that the card players hoped that the baby would wake up and would have to be taken into the living room. Franz saw none of this: In his own eyes he had become an "outsider" to his family, an outsider who hadn't ever left his home.

In his voluminous, soon daily, correspondence with Felice Bauer, Franz would often mention his parents, mostly to stress his lack of feelings for both father and mother; on this topic, however, the letters are unreliable, as Kafka wanted to convince Felice that she was the only person he loved and was capable of loving. At the same time, he hoped to convey to her how unfit he was for family life. On both sides, though, families and friends were informed of the relationship and on both sides they welcomed it, as background and social status seemed to fit.

While he expressed his antagonism to the family in the letters to Felice, Franz described his father's outbursts rather as a mere "show" in a letter to his sister Ottla, in April 1917.[21] Moreover, as objectively as this antagonism can be judged, one does not perceive any grievous offense from Hermann's side, beyond the minor irritations unavoidably part of the relations between parents and children (and mainly between father and son, especially if their personality traits differ as thoroughly as they did between Hermann and Franz). In part, Hermann's well-intentioned financial help to Franz and, later, to Ottla— although one may wonder why Franz would have needed it— created, as Franz wrote to Ottla at the end of December 1917, a constant dependence by the two of them on their father.[22] To Franz this dependence, that he could have easily shaken off, was insufferable, but he continued to accept it nonetheless. Would it disappear when transposed into fiction? Franz believed that in his writings he would free himself from his father . . .

3

"Here," in the writings, Franz pointed out in the "Letter,"

I had, in fact, got some distance away from you by my own efforts, even if it was slightly reminiscent of the worm that, when a foot treads on its tail end, breaks loose with its front part and drags itself aside. To a certain extent I was in safety; there was a chance to breathe freely. The aversion you naturally and immediately took to my writing was, for once, welcome to me. My vanity, my ambition did suffer under your soon proverbial way of hailing the arrival of my books: "Put it on my bedside table!" (usually you were playing cards when a book came), but I was really quite glad of it, not only out of rebellious malice, not only out of delight at a new confirmation of my view of our relationship, but quite spontaneously, because to me that formula sounded something like: "Now you are free!" Of course it was a delusion; I was not, or, to put it most optimistically, was not yet, free. My writing was all about you; all I did there, after all, was to bemoan what I could not bemoan upon your breast. It was an intentionally long and drawn-out leave-taking from you, yet, although it was enforced by you, it did take its course in the direction determined by me.[23]

In the "Letter," Franz allows for (not unconvincing) rejoinders from Hermann but, of course, keeps the last word, a last word that shows again the depth of his own hate-love attitude: "This whole rejoinder—which can partly also be turned against you—does not come from you, but from me. . . . I do not deny a certain justification for this rejoinder, which in itself contributes new material to the characterization of our relationship. Naturally things cannot in reality fit together the way the evidence does in my letter; life is more than a Chinese puzzle. But with the correction made by this rejoinder—a correction I neither can nor will elaborate in detail—in my opinion something has been achieved which so closely approximates the truth that it might reassure us both a little and make our living and our dying easier."[24]

In reality things did not fit together as they did in the "Letter," nor did they fit like a Chinese puzzle in Franz's fiction, either. Could it be that the stories and the novels expressed a level of complexity in the relations between father and son, originating in the deepest recesses of Kafka's mind, that he himself had not entirely grasped?

Before turning to the three emblematic stories about the relations between the sons and their fathers that Kafka wished to see published in one volume as *The Sons*, but that were ultimately published as three separate texts—"The Stoker," "The Judgment," and *The Metamorphosis*—let me venture a remark about Kafka's three great novels. In the first, *Amerika*, or *The Man Who Disappeared*, Karl, the protagonist, is expelled by his family at the very outset of the story, and will never see his parents again (this, in fact, is the basic theme of "The Stoker," the first chapter of the novel); in *The Trial*, Joseph K. considers, at some point, the vague project to visit his old mother, but the plan doesn't bode well as the mother has supposedly become very religious and is possibly somewhat senile (that chapter was not completed, and Kafka's intention remains unknown); of a father, there is no mention and no trace. Finally, in *The Castle*, K. mentions vaguely the town in which he was born, its church, and the cemetery wall he once climbed, but about parents, no word is uttered. Such absence may be as meaningful as the disastrous presence of the families in "The Judgment" and *The Metamorphosis*.

"The Judgment," written during the night of September 22–23, 1912, marked an entirely new phase in Kafka's creativity. Georg, the son, decides to carry his old father from his usual room, dark even on a sunny day, to the front room where, until the furniture is moved, he can lie in the son's bed. "He carried his father over to the bed in his arms. It gave him a dreadful feeling to observe that while he was taking the few steps toward the bed, the old man cradled against his chest was playing with his watch chain . . ."[25]

The childlike old father is put down in the new bed and carefully covered with blankets; with senile anxiety, he asks whether he is well covered, and twice the son reassures him: "Don't worry, you're well covered up." But, then: "'No!' cried the father, so that the answer collided with the question, and flinging the blanket back so violently that for a moment it hovered unfolded in the air, he stood upright in bed. With one hand he lightly touched the ceiling to steady himself. "You wanted to cover me up, I know, my little puppy, but I'm far from being covered up. And even if this is the last bit of strength I have, it's enough for you, more than enough."[26] The resurrected father condemns his son to death; the son obeys, rushes out, jumps from a bridge, and drowns himself.

In *The Metamorphosis*, the father also "resurrects," and ultimately what follows leads to the son's death, as in "The Judgment." While Gregor Samsa was still the proud breadwinner for the entire family, the father did not work, following some financial mishap. "In the old days [he] used to lie wearily buried in bed when Gregor left on a business trip; [he] greeted him on his return in the evening, sitting in his bathrobe in the armchair [and] actually had difficulty getting to his feet but as a sign of joy could only lift up his arms . . ."[27]

But on the fateful day when Gregor ventures into the family living room just as his father returns from his new job, the son cannot believe his eyes: "Now, the father was holding himself very erect, dressed in a tight-fitting blue uniform with gold buttons, the kind worn by messengers at banking concerns; above the high stiff color of the jacket, his heavy chin protruded; under his bushy eyebrows, his black eyes darted bright, piercing glances; his usually crumpled white hair was combed flat, with a scrupulously exact, gleaming part."[28]

The resurrected fathers (or simply, the fathers) hound the sons to their death. Death here can be interpreted in many figurative ways. The most obvious is castration. In his "Letter," Franz came close to such a reading: "Being what we are, marrying is barred to me because it is your very own domain. . . . The desire for marriage was powerless for other reasons. Those lay in your relation to your children, which is, after all what this whole letter is about."[29]

In his interpretation of *The Metamorphosis*, Eric Santner sees the resurrected fathers as retaining traces of their previous weakness within their reborn power: "One of the most uncanny features of Kafka's literary universe is doubtless the way in which such impotence can suddenly reverse itself into awesome power, or better, the way in which impotence reveals itself to be one of the most disturbing attributes of power."[30] However, if the fathers' power was still marred by weakness, the fathers would at some point show hesitation about the use of their new strength. In "The Judgment," there is no sign of paternal hesitation; in *The Metamorphosis*, the father asks wife and daughter what can be done with Gregor but then relents immediately when Gregor's sister lashes out. Is that moment a sign of weakness? Hardly: the events have to follow the most extreme course, and, in this case, the parents and their daughter act as one unit (the "family" against which Franz will inveigh at times), and throughout the text, the father remains the supreme authority within that unit. This becomes utterly clear when, toward the end, father Samsa expels the three lodgers: "At that point the bedroom door opened, and Mr. Samsa appeared in his uniform, his wife on one arm, his daughter on the other. . . .

'Leave my house immediately,' said Mr. Samsa and pointed to the door, without letting go of the women."[31]

Seen as a whole, these texts show a merciless link between the fathers' power, the sexual awakening of the sons, and their castration/death. In "The Judgment," Georg becomes engaged to a Fräulein Frieda Brandenfeld (her initials suggest Felice Bauer, the young woman Kafka met a short time before writing the story); the father intervenes and condemns his son to death. In *The Metamorphosis*, the son's sexual awakening leads to a double confrontation with the father: first a classically Freudian oedipal struggle, then implicitly following Gregor's incestuous longing for his sister.

The oedipal struggle takes place when the mother sees her son's animality and faints outright in Gregor's room. Kafka gives an ambiguous rendition of mother Samsa's fainting. "As if giving up completely, she fell with outstretched arms across the couch and did not stir." Whatever the case may be, the mother flees to the living room, shedding her clothes on the way, and unites in embrace with the father. The father then throws the fatal apple at his oedipal rival; it will ultimately lead to Gregor's death.

The second episode is more protracted and involves two separate texts. In *The Metamorphosis*, the second paragraph of the story already announces Gregor Samsa's sexual awakening: "His room, a regular human bedroom, only a little on the small side, lay quiet between the four familiar walls. Over the table, on which an unpacked line of fabric samples was all spread out—Samsa was traveling salesman—hung the picture which he had recently cut out of a glossy magazine and lodged into a pretty gilt frame. It showed a lady done up in a fur hat and a fur boa, sitting upright and raising up against the viewer a heavy fur muff in which her whole forearm had disappeared."[32] *Venus in Furs* was the title of Leopold von Sacher-Masoch's classic novel of sadomasochism; and, in Gregor's room, the woman clad in furs "holding to the spectator a huge fur muff" appears as a symbol of feminine sexuality and sexual enticement. It is the picture that Gregor will attempt, in vain, to defend against his mother and sister later in the story.

Ottla, Kafka's youngest sister, was always closest to him. Yet during the period he was writing *The Metamorphosis* and then *The Trial*, Franz suspected that Ottla had taken his father's side in their contentions. Love and "treason" appear in the strange similarity between excerpts of both texts. Although *The Trial* was written two years after *The Metamorphosis*, it confirms the sexual meaning of the same incriminating episode.

In *The Trial*, Joseph K.'s first interrogation takes place not in his own room but in that of a Fräulein Bürstner, his neighbor, then away at work. In the evening Joseph K. wants to tell the Fräulein (who usually returns late) what happened. He lays in wait for her, enters her room and manages to tell his story, but, as she pushes him out of the room, he "seized her, and kissed her first on the lips, then all over the face, like some thirsty animal lapping greedily at a spring of long-sought fresh water. Finally he kissed her on the neck, right on the throat and kept his lips there for a long time . . ."[33]

As for Gregor the bug, he dreamed about his sister, who so beautifully played the violin, about keeping her with him forever:

> He would never again let her out of his room—at least not for as long as he lived; for once, his nightmarish looks would be of use to him; he would be at all the doors of his room at the same time and hiss and spit at the aggressors; his sister, however, should not be forced to stay with him, but would do so of her own free will; she should sit still next to him on the couch, bending her ear down to him, and then he would confide to her that he had had the firm intention of sending her to the Conservatory and that, if the catastrophe had not intervened, he would have announced this to everyone with-

out allowing any objection. After this declaration, his sister would burst into tears of emotion, and Gregor would raise himself up to her shoulder and kiss her on the neck which, ever since she started going out to work, she kept bare, without a ribbon or collar.[34]

The concluding sequence of Gregor's pining for his sister follows a few days later. The Samsas have rented a room to three tenants, and one evening the daughter accepts their invitation to play the violin for them. At the sound of his sister's playing, Gregor cannot help moving into the living room. He is seen; havoc ensues and he hardly manages to make it back to his room. This time, however, the sister joins the father's camp, in fact she takes over; Gregor must be disposed of: "'It has to go,' cried the sister, 'that's the only answer, Father.'"[35] Gregor hears it all and, increasingly paralyzed by the apple stuck in his back, he is rapidly approaching his end. The father had struck the fatal blow; the sister has added her treacherous desire for Gregor's death to keep her own life unfettered.

What went through Kafka's mind as he wrote the last part of *The Metamorphosis* we don't know. Could it have been above and beyond fantasies of incest and castration, an urge to parody Sophocles' *Antigone?* Here the sister, instead of standing up against the father and king in order to bury her slain brother as in the Greek tragedy, takes the lead in getting rid of him and lets the cleaning lady throw away his remains like any other garbage.

But are the death sentences, is the castration the possible result of some hidden sin the sons may have committed, that would justify, given their own meek reactions, the violence of the paternal verdict? The answer is barely hinted at in the stories (except, maybe, regarding Gregor's incestuous urges), but it could have been Kafka's secret subtext. Sexual self-assertion was not only forbidden to the sons, it was twice forbidden if, as was the case, it was a banned form of sexual desire, one that the father, the carrier of accepted bourgeois social norms, would never admit. Georg in "The Judgment" mentions his engagement to Frieda Brandenfeld, but as Franz knows, F.B., whom he had recently met, could be an epistolary confidante at best, not a real bride. He was about to lie to Felice, to his parents, and to "society."

In *The Metamorphosis*, Gregor's unclean (sinful) nature is asserted in the very first sentence, where the German *ungeheures Ungeziefer* is translated by Stanley Corngold as "monstrous vermin," instead of "gigantic insect," as in the standard English rendition. Corngold writes, regarding the negative sense of this initial identification: "*Ungeziefer* derives (as Kafka probably knew) from the late Middle High German word originally meaning 'the unclean animal not suited for sacrifice.'"[36]

Thus there may be some plausible interpretation of the ambivalence of feelings of the condemned sons about their tyrannical fathers' sentences: above and beyond an oedipal conflict, they know of a sin that the fathers ignore but that they, the sons, have to expiate.

Georg Bendemann's last words in "The Judgment," as, following his father's verdict, he jumps to his death, are: "Dear Parents, I have always loved you, all the same."[37] In *The Metamorphosis* the scene repeats itself. After the fatally wounded Gregor Samsa has been driven back into his room for a third time: "He thought back on his family with deep emotion and love. . . . Then, without his consent, his head sank down to the floor, and from his nostrils streamed his last weak breath."[38] The son's submission and self-sacrifice appears again in "In the Penal Colony," written at the same time as *The Metamorphosis* and just before *The Trial*; but in that story, there is no ambivalence: father and son are one.

"In the Penal Colony" describes the visit by an explorer to what appears to be a French penal colony set on an island (possibly an allusion to Devil's Island, where Captain Alfred Drey-fus had been exiled after his condemnation). During the visit the explorer has to witness an execution and give his opinion on keeping or abolishing a procedure invented by the "Old Com-mandant" of the island. The condemned man (usually a native soldier sentenced without trial) perishes as the steel needles of a special machine engrave the verdict into his flesh. The un-folding of the story derives from the devotion of the officer in charge of the machine (and of the executions) to the legacy of the Old Commandant, dead for several years. Although the New Commandant is hostile to the torture—and seemingly plans to end it—the officer in charge considers it his sacred duty to maintain this tradition and, in general, keep the rules set by the Old Commandant. Thus when he discovers that the explorer will not support him, he frees the condemned soldier from his shackles, lies on the "bed" of the machine, sets it in motion and is killed by it.

In "The Judgment," *The Metamorphosis*, and "In the Penal Colony," the sons are driven to their death by the father. In "In the Penal Colony," we can safely surmise that the Old Com-mandant considered the officer as his disciple, as the one who would carry on his teachings and keep his decrees. When faced with his imminent failure to do so, the officer proclaims his own guilt by choosing self-immolation.

"In the Penal Colony" does not end with the officer's sui-cide. After the officer's death, the explorer, a soldier, and the previously condemned man walk from the execution site to the town and stop at the Teahouse. At that point, the soldier in-forms the other two that "the old man's buried here."

They enter, one of the tables is pushed aside, and the grave-stone appears; the inscription reads: "Here rests the Old Com-mandant. His adherents, who now must be nameless, have dug this grave and set up this stone. There is a prophecy that after a certain number of years the Commandant will rise again and lead his adherents from this house to recover the colony. Have faith and wait!'"[39]

This time, however, the resurrection is not meant to threaten a hated or despised son but to rescue and empower a dutifully obedient and devoted spiritual son. Except, of course, for the fact that this son is already dead, a martyr to his "father's" cause; dead due to the shame and the guilt produced by his inability to save the father's quasi-religious heritage; dead because of the father's (imagined) injunction to defend the tradition.

The difference in the sons' "transgression" and punishment between "The Judgment" and *The Metamorphosis* on the one hand and "In the Penal Colony" on the other may be read as an evolution in the symbolic significance of paternal authority from its most fundamental psychosexual function (in a Freudian sense) to its preeminent social function as representing tradition and the law. In the first two stories, the living father is the only authority, and the sons meekly accept their fate due to their ambivalence of feelings and sense of guilt. In the third story, the power of decision is transferred from father to son, but this power is an illusion, as the son cannot know what the law requires; he can merely guess, and his readiness for self-immolation is based solely on shame and guilt. In that sense, "In the Penal Colony" marks a transition to Kafka's later texts, beginning with *The Trial*, in which the source of the authority, the nature of the law, and its rules of implementation remain hidden to the end.

Most commentators have taken Franz's relations with his family as a given that did not demand much pondering. For some, however, particularly for Peter-André Alt, whose massive biography carries the telling subtitle *Der ewige Sohn* (probably best translated as "Forever the Son"), Franz's attitude toward his father was essential. In Alt's words, Kafka "cultivated his fear of the father with obsessive pleasure, because it was for him the very condition of his existence." In refusing to grow up, in failing to face the major challenges of adult life (full-fledged relationships, marriage, fatherhood, and the like), Kafka was creating, thanks to his childlike dependency, his own space, the necessary condition for the writer's life.[40]

There is no way of reconstructing the psychological dynamics that led Kafka to "cultivate" his fear of the father and his ambivalent antagonism. Alt's hypothesis is plausible although it cannot avoid a minor hurdle: Franz's anger crystallized and turned into the notorious "Letter" not when the parents favored his outward readiness to get married (they welcomed Felice Bauer but did not intervene beyond the customary niceties) but when the father opposed the son's marriage plans to Julie Wohryzek. What should have secretly pleased Kafka, if we follow Alt's assumption, led on the contrary to his explosive response.

One could introduce a slight variation: Franz, knowingly or not, stoked partly fictitious grievances, wallowed in the ensuing family dramas not only because it fed his notorious masochism but also—and mainly—because, symbolically at least, it established his *difference* from surrounding society. Franz, well aware of the father's weaknesses and of his irascible nature, subtly took upon himself the role of toreador in a lifelong corrida, meant as the secret assertion of his own particular self.

2

"The Dark Complexity of Judaism"

"You ask me if I am a Jew," Kafka wrote to Milena Jesenska in May 1920, soon after the beginning of their correspondence. "Perhaps this is only a joke, perhaps you are only asking me if I belong to those anxious Jews, in any case as a native of Prague you can't be as innocent in this respect as Mathilde, Heinrich Heine's wife." Thereupon, Kafka tells Milena the amusing story of this very naïve Mathilde (Mirat), who was convinced that Heine's friends in Paris were all Germans — and she did not like any of them (Heine himself was a converted Jew). When she was told by a non-Jewish friend that they were all journalists and all Jews, she didn't believe it and asked about each of them and in each case was told that this one, and this one too, were Jews. "Finally, Mathilde got annoyed and said: 'You're trying to tease me; in the end you will even make out that Kohn is a Jewish name, but Kohn after all is Henry's [Heine's] cousin and Henry is a Lutheran!'"[1]

Of course Milena, herself married to the Prague Jew Ernst Pollak, must have known that Kafka was a Jew; her question could have been meant as a joke or possibly as a way of asking: "What kind of Jew are you?," maybe not as Kafka assumed ("those anxious Jews") but rather: "What does it mean for you: being Jewish?" These hypothetical questions were the ones that, in any number of variations, Kafka himself attempted to answer throughout his life.

I

During the second half of the nineteenth century, a majority of middle-class Jews living in the cities of Central Europe (mainly Berlin, Vienna, and Prague) were adopting the values of an increasingly secularized surrounding society. In Prague particularly, it meant keeping religious obligations to a strict (and often purely formulaic) minimum: observing the High Holidays, having a Seder meal on Passover eve, and keeping some traditional practices of Jewish life (circumcision, Bar Mitzvah, religious weddings and funerals) for "the sake of piety," according to father Kafka.

In fact, Jewish "assimilation," as it was called—the trend toward secularism—knew many degrees and various national models. Everywhere in the West, however, notwithstanding the Heines or the Disraelis, most Jews choosing that path didn't walk the one further stretch through the gates of conversion. As a well-known French Jewish socialite quipped: "I have too little religion to change it."[2] The result, of course, led to maintaining a Jewish identity without knowing why. For Hermann Kafka's generation, this was no problem. For Franz's generation—more precisely for some young Jewish intellectuals of that cohort—such meaninglessness seemed unacceptable.

A majority of the younger cohort did nonetheless accept assimilation (mainly without conversion). This often led to paradoxical behavior (wittily described by the Viennese Jewish author Arthur Schnitzler in his 1908 novel *Der Weg ins Freie* [*The Road into the Open*]): imitation of all social mannerisms of surrounding Gentile society and yet the need to proclaim on every possible occasion that one was a Jew.[3]

In Kafka's group of friends, for those who searched alternatives to passive assimilation, the choices were quite well defined: keeping or returning to religion, as in the case of Hugo Bergmann and later of Max Brod (and in an extreme form, in the case of another Kafka friend, Georg Langer, who became, for a few years, an ultra-Orthodox follower of the Hasidic Belzer Rebbe), or fervent commitment to the newly established Zionist movement (Bergmann, Brod, Weltsch), or both. In Eastern Europe, adhesion to a Jewish socialist movement (Bund), established in 1905, Yiddishist, anti-Zionist, and supporting a measure of Jewish cultural and national autonomy in the Diaspora, became one of the most successful options; in Central and Western Europe, Jews often became active in local socialist parties, although the Bund had some adherents as well, mainly among immigrants from the East. There has been and there still is much discussion about Kafka's active socialism; I will return to it later. Various esoteric quests also appeared as open paths, and so did, rarely, but as happened with one of Franz's uncles, Rudolph, conversion.[4] Finally, there was departure for the "land of all wonders": America.

Franz kept his distance both from religion and from Zionism. Nonetheless, in the "Letter," he did not miss berating his father for the feeble religious tradition he had passed on to him: "As a child I reproached myself, in accord with you, for not going to the synagogue often enough, for not fasting and so on. I thought that in this way I was doing a wrong not to myself but to you, and I was penetrated by a sense of guilt, which was, of course, always near at hand."[5]

However, the son recognized the wider social context of

this dwindling of belief and tradition: "You really had brought some traces of Judaism with you from the ghetto-like village community; it was not much and it dwindled a little more in the city and during your military service. . . . The whole thing is, of course, no isolated phenomenon. It was much the same with a large section of this transitional generation of Jews, which had migrated from the still comparatively devout countryside to the cities . . ."[6]

In an oft-quoted letter to Brod, written in June 1921, Franz established a further link between the lack of commitment to Jewishness of his father's generation and the problems encountered by those sons who wanted to be writers (staying Jews in a meaningful way or leaving Judaism): "Most young Jews who wanted to write German wanted to leave Jewishness behind them, and their fathers approved of this, but vaguely (this vagueness was what was outrageous to them). But with their posterior legs they were still glued to their father's Jewishness and with their waving anterior legs they found no new ground. The ensuing despair became their inspiration."[7]

Franz remembered his own Bar Mitzvah (his parents called it "confirmation") as the learning by heart of some incomprehensible text, delivering some meaningless speech (also learned by heart), and that was it. Although during his last high school years, he apparently debated the existence of God with his schoolmate Hugo Bergmann (Bergmann believed, Kafka did not), Jewishness does not seem to have been on his mind at that time, except for venturing a few nasty remarks about Jewish clerks to his Jewish friend, Oskar Pollak: "Today is Sunday," he wrote to him in November 1903, "when the clerks always come down Wenzelsplatz across the Graben and clamor for Sunday quiet [should be "rest"]. I think their red carnations and their stupid and Jewish faces and their clamor is something highly significant."[8]

Yet when it came to social life, to intellectual exchanges,

and, almost always, to emotional life as well, Kafka steadily remained within the confines of a Jewish environment. And as the years went by, he became increasingly attuned to "Jewishness," even before the major change about to come. Thus, during his second tour with Brod through neighboring countries in early September 1911, he attempted on several occasions to guess whether a passenger in his train compartment was Jewish, or he mentioned Brod's comments on Jews (a habit shared, for opposite reasons of course, by Jews and antisemites).[9] The significant turning point occurred in October 1911, on the occasion of the visit to Prague of the Yiddish theater from Lemberg in Polish Galicia, at the time a part of the Austro-Hungarian Empire.

"Last night Café Savoy. Yiddish troupe," Kafka noted on October 5 in the diary he had started the previous year. "Some songs, the expression '*Yiddische kinderlach*,' some of this woman's acting [the actress K. in Lateiner's play *Der Meshumed*, "The Apostate"]—who, on the stage, because she is a Jew, draws us listeners to her because we are Jews, without any longing for or curiosity about Christians—made my cheeks tremble . . ."[10]

Kafka's enthusiasm lasted (although he was well aware of the mediocre quality of the performances) mostly due to the unfettered Jewishness of these Yiddish actors, as they played their Jewish roles and lived their unquestioned Jewish lives. They were "authentic" Eastern European Jews, the absolute contrast to being Jewish in his surroundings, particularly in his father's surroundings.

Indeed, Hermann Kafka did not appreciate in the least his son's sudden enthusiasm for what Hermann considered as uneducated and primitive Jews. He was particularly annoyed about Franz's friendship with the young manager of the theater company, Yitzhak Löwy, and did not hesitate to express his feelings in front of his son, as Franz reminded him in the

"Letter": "Without knowing him [Löwy], you compared him, in some dreadful way that I have now forgotten, to vermin and, as was so often the case with people I was fond of, you were automatically ready with the proverb of the dog and its fleas."[11] Hermann, of course, had his good reasons for sneering at Franz's newfound infatuation: while the son was welcoming a new, more vital Judaism, the father wanted to safeguard at all costs the achievements of assimilation.

On February 18, 1912, Kafka gave a public lecture on Yiddish (*Einleitungsvortrag über Jargon*) to introduce Löwy's reading of short texts from Yiddish literature: Franz's parents did not attend.[12]

Franz's enthusiastic reaction to the Yiddish theater group greatly reinforced his interest in Jewish issues. But he recognized that the Eastern Jewish "authenticity," as admirable as it was in its context, could not be simply transposed to his own Jewish world, that of Central and Western Europe. And his keener attention to the Jewish environment in which he lived brought up a critical attitude that, at times, turned into sarcastic comments influenced by some of the antisemitic slurs of those years.

Thus, at the end of May 1921, Kafka wrote to Brod from a sanatorium in Matliary, in the Tatra mountains: "If the world shouts a ghoulish cry into my grave-like peace, then I fly off the handle and beat my forehead against the door of madness that is always unlatched. A trifle is enough to bring me to this state. It is enough if under my balcony, his face turned toward me, a young half-pious Hungarian Jew in his reclining chair, comfortably outstretched with one hand over his head, the other thrust deep into his fly, all day long cheerfully keeps on humming temple melodies. (What a people!)."[13]

The aversion to the uncouth Jew is, here and there, tainted by aversion to the "Jewish type." The tone remains facetious, but the remarks cannot be entirely dismissed: "I am thriving among all the animals," Kafka wrote to Elsa and Max Brod at the beginning of October 1917, from Zürau, a village where he was staying at his sister Ottla's home in an attempt to regain some health. "This afternoon I fed goats. . . . These goats, by the way, look like thoroughly Jewish types, mostly doctors, though there are a few approximations of lawyers, Polish Jews, and a scattering of pretty girls in the flock. Dr W., the doctor who treats me, is heavily represented among them . . ."[14]

As Sander Gilman has pointed out, Kafka was ashamed of his body as a typical Jewish body, characterized in the antisemitic imagination of the time by various defects and disgraceful characteristics; the Jewish male body in particular was seen as effeminate and weak (ill). "Kafka," writes Gilman, "is quite aware of the power of the argument about the feminization of the male Jew. . . . The acculturated Jew is fated to become ill, effeminate, and sterile."[15]

This indeed was a common antisemitic stereotype (applied no less to Eastern European Jews than to acculturated Western ones), particularly widespread in German-speaking countries as an integral part of racial antisemitism. In Austria, at the turn of the century Otto Weininger's best-selling *Geschlecht und Charakter* (*Sex and Character*) boosted the stereotype by equating Jews with women in a peculiar antisemitic and misogynist view of the world.[16] "Women and Jews did not possess a rational and moral self and, therefore, neither deserved nor needed equality with Aryan men or even simple liberty."[17] Both psychically and biologically the Jew was feminine and effeminate. Incidentally, Weininger was a Jew converted to Protestantism; he published his book in 1903, at age twenty-three and, soon after, committed suicide.[18] There is little doubt that Kafka had read Weininger, although he mentions him but fleetingly by asking his friend Oskar Baum for a copy of the lecture he had given about *Sex and Character*.[19] In Franz's circle, Weininger's

45

theories about women and about Jews were common knowledge.

It is also plausible that Kafka did not remain indifferent to the antisemitic slurs about the effeminate Jewish body, not only because of doubts about his own sexual identity, or the earlier physical humiliation felt when, as a child, he accompanied his father to the swimming pool, or as a result of his own chronic physical ailments, but also because his Zionist friends were themselves contemptuous of the Diaspora Jew's physique, intent as they were to create a "new Jew" (a "muscular Jew" in Max Nordau's well-known expression) in Eretz Israel.[20]

Nonetheless, Kafka did not internalize the main anti-semitic corollary: the wiping out of the Jew's identity, the self-immolation of Jewishness. He came close to that red line in one outburst only, in a letter to Milena, to whom he wrote on June 13, 1920: "I could . . . reproach you for having much too high an opinion of the Jews whom you do know (me included) — there are others! — at times I would like to stuff them all, simply as Jews (me included) into, say, the drawer of the laundry chest. Next I'd wait, open the drawer a little to see if they have all suffocated, and if not, shut the drawer again and keep doing this to the end."[21] Apart from this extreme example — and nothing close to it ever reappeared in Kafka's correspondence or in his diaries — his negative remarks about Jews almost always surfaced in letters to Jewish friends, which gives them a very different significance from what they would mean otherwise.

As for Kafka's musings about his lack of identification with other Jews, they didn't mean more than moments of discouragement not necessarily related to Jews but rather to himself, to himself in the world. Thus sounds the best known of such comments, which he wrote in January 1914: "What have I in common with Jews? I have hardly anything in common with myself and should stand very quietly in a corner, content that I can breathe . . ."[22]

Besides such chance remarks, Kafka had more serious and sustained arguments about the political and cultural role of Western Jews in their societies, particularly in postwar Germany. "Perhaps the Jews are not spoiling Germany's future," he wrote to Brod, in May 1920, "but it is possible to conceive of them as having spoiled Germany's present. From early on they have forced upon Germany things that she might have arrived at slowly and in her own way, but which she was opposed to because they stemmed from strangers. What a barren preoccupation Anti-Semitism is, everything that goes with it, and Germany owes that to her Jews."[23]

This comment came in response to Brod's remarks about "Munich"—probably to the prominent role played by a few leaders of Jewish origin in the Communist uprising that took place there in the last days of February 1919 and led to the setting up of a short-lived "republic of the councils" in the city. These events did indeed exacerbate an already deep hatred on the German right against Jews, especially once the ground had been prepared by the defeat of 1918, the establishment of the Weimar Republic, and the spread in postwar Germany of a poisonous antisemitic propaganda holding the Jews responsible for all sufferings and national humiliations.

Kafka was no less critical of Jewish contributions—questionable, in his view—to German culture. In the June 1921 letter to Brod, he stressed that Jews were "irresistibly attracted" to German language and culture, a culture that, according to him, did not belong to them. This situation led Jewish writers to four impossibilities:

> The impossibility of not writing, the impossibility of writing in German, the impossibility of writing differently. One

might also add a fourth impossibility, the impossibility of writing (since the despair could not be assuaged by writing, was hostile to both life and writing; writing is only an expedient, as for someone who is writing his will shortly before he hangs himself—an expedient that may well last a whole life). Thus what resulted was a literature impossible in all respects, a gipsy literature that had stolen the German child out of his cradle and in great haste put it through some kind of training, for someone has to dance on the tightrope. (But it wasn't even a German child, it was nothing; people merely said that somebody was dancing) . . .[24]

Kafka was in fact joining a debate that for years had agitated quite a few German Jews and, well beyond, had been a major theme of modern antisemitism. In the eyes of most European antisemites, the Jews, by getting involved in the culture of their "adoptive" countries, were meddling with a national heritage to which they were quintessentially foreign and thus were perverting and undermining that heritage, whether intentionally or not. Some Jews, particularly in Germany, had taken up that argument, and at times had accepted the idea that they were participating in a culture in which they were unwanted. Some even accepted the conclusion which a Jewish journalist, Moritz Goldstein, had propounded in a notorious essay in Ferdinand Avenarius's *Der Kunstwart* in 1912: Jews should abandon the dream of participating in German cultural life and, instead, turn inward to their own Jewish cultural heritage; others went farther and pushed for a return to Jewish cultural roots—not in Germany, though, or anywhere else in the Diaspora, but in Eretz Israel, where an authentic Hebrew culture would be revived and could flourish again.

Of course, Kafka understood that, seen from such an angle, the cultural identity of his own writings was as confusing for others as it was for himself. Thus in October 1916 he wrote to Felice: "And incidentally won't you tell me what I really am.

In the last *Neue Rundschau*, 'Metamorphosis' is mentioned and rejected on sensible grounds, and then says the writer: 'There is something fundamentally German about K's narrative art.' In Max's article on the other hand [published in *Der Jude*]: 'K's stories are among the most typically Jewish documents of our time.'" Whereupon Kafka added an oft-mentioned quip: "A difficult case. Am I a circus rider on 2 horses? Alas, I am no rider, but lie prostrate on the ground."[25]

2

Notwithstanding all the confusion and the criticism, Kafka felt Jewish to the marrow of his bones. As he noted in his diary in December 1911, "In Hebrew my name is Anschel, like my mother's maternal grandfather, whom my mother, who was six years old when he died, can remember as a very pious and learned man with a long, white beard . . ."[26]

All of Kafka's literary friends, his entire circle in Prague and beyond, were Jews: Oskar Pollak and Hugo Bergmann at first, then Max Brod, Felix Weltsch, Willy Haas, Ernst Weiss, Oskar Baum, Franz Werfel, Georg Langer, and, later still, Robert Klopstock. Most of the women he felt close to—the two exceptions being a Swiss girl he briefly met in a sanatorium in Riva and, of course, Milena Jesenska—were Jewish: Hedwig Weiler, Felice Bauer, Grete Bloch, Julie Wohryzek, Minze Eisner, Dora Diamant. Thus Kafka's immersion in a predominantly Jewish milieu, throughout his life (except again for his workplace, which he constantly dreamt of leaving)—and the absence of any indication that he wished to put that milieu behind him—clearly outlines the social context of a personal identity he was desperately trying to define and nourish.

While Kafka's enthusiasm for the Yiddish theater was waxing, he started reading voraciously about Jewish topics. "Today," he recorded on November 1, 1911, "eagerly and happily began to read the *History of the Jews* by Graetz. Because my desire for it had far outrun the reading, it was at first stranger to me than I thought, and I had to stop here and there in order by resting to allow my Jewishness to collect itself."[27]

A few weeks later, in early January 1912, he was so taken by Meir Isser Pines's *L'Histoire de la littérature Judéo-allemande* that he didn't even find time for his diary: "For the following reasons have not written for so long," he noted on January 24: "read, and indeed greedily, Pines' *L'Histoire de la littérature Judéo-allemande*, 500 pages, with such thoroughness, haste, and joy as I have never yet shown in the case of similar books; now I am reading Fromer, *Organismus des Judentums . . .*"[28] His delight in Pines's volume led him to transcribe extensive information from it to his diary: Jewish soldiers' songs, sayings from rabbinic literature, short biographies of Yiddish writers, summaries of some main themes in I. L. Peretz's and Shalom Aleichem's stories and, of course, various details of Jewish history.[29]

Unexpectedly, though, Kafka disliked the best-known Western literary attempt to convey the gist of Hasidic spirituality: Martin Buber's *Tales of Hasidism* and *The Legend of the Baal Shem*. On January 16, 1913, he wrote to Felice: "Buber is lecturing on the Jewish myth; it would take more than Buber to get me out of my room, I have heard him before, I find him dreary; no matter what he says, something is missing . . ."[30] A few days later he returned to the subject and mentioned that it could have been the "drastic adaptation" Buber made of the Hasidic texts "that makes his book of legends so intolerable to me."[31] (Later he came to appreciate Buber adaptations of Hasidic stories, such as *Der Grosse Magid*, among others.)

Generally, Kafka liked the Jewish folklore from Eastern Europe, as he wrote to Brod, at the end of September 1917: "The Hasidic stories in *Jüdisches Echo* may not be the best, but for some reason I don't understand, all these stories are the only Jewish literature in which I immediately and always feel at home, quite apart from my own state of mind. With all the rest I am only wafted in and another draught wafts me out again. I will keep the stories for a while, if you have no objection."[32]

The attraction to Hasidism did not reach beyond literature, however, as is clear from Kafka's comments on his visit to the Belzer Rebbe, arranged by his Orthodox friend Georg Langer while the Rebbe was staying in Marienbad. "All in all," he wrote to Brod, in July 1916, "what comes from him [the Rebbe] are the inconsequential comments and questions of itinerant royalty, perhaps somewhat more childish and more joyous. At any rate they reduce all thinking on the part of his escort to the same level. Langer tries to find or thinks he finds a deeper meaning in all this; I think that the deeper meaning is that there is none and in my opinion this is quite enough."[33]

How, then, could the Judaism to which Kafka belonged redeem itself, become authentic? To define the nature of such "authenticity" was not easy, and Kafka, in some of his letters to Felice, had to remain rather vague when, for example, comparing Western and Eastern Jewry. At the end of 1916, Felice was to start working at the Home for Jewish Children (mainly children of Eastern European families) established in Berlin that May; Kafka strongly encouraged her project and repeatedly commented about it. What was the nature of the education that "the helpers" (teachers) were supposed to instill, Kafka asked rhetorically, and answered with some measure of irony:

> One will try to raise them [the children] to the standard of the contemporary, educated West European Jew, Berlin version, which admittedly may be the best type of its kind. With that, not much would be achieved. If, for instance, I had to choose between the Berlin Home and another where

the pupils were the Berlin helpers . . . and the helpers simple
East European Jews from Kolomyja or Stanislawow, I would
give unconditional preference to the latter Home. . . . The
quality corresponding to the value of the East European Jew
is something that cannot be imparted in a Home. . . . These
are things that cannot be imparted, but perhaps, and here
lies the hope, they can be acquired, earned. And the helpers
in the Home have, I imagine, a chance to acquire them. . . .
They [the helpers] will accomplish little, for they know little
and are not very bright, yet once they grasp the meaning
of it, they will accomplish all they can with all their hearts,
which on the other hand is a lot, this alone is a lot.[34]

Regarding his religious position, Kafka expressed himself
with utmost clarity in another 1916 letter to Felice about work
with the Berlin children:

On the whole it will be up to you to get them [the children]
to trust you in other than religious matters and, where the
religious experience is needed, to let the dark complexity of
Judaism, which contains so many impenetrable features, do
its work. . . . While I should have to tell the children . . .
that owing to my origin, my education, disposition and environment I have nothing tangible in common with their faith
(keeping the Commandments is not an outward thing; on
the contrary, it is the very essence of the Jewish faith)—thus
while I would somehow have to admit it to them, you, on the
other hand, may not be altogether lacking in tangible con-
nections with the faith . . .[35]

For the sake of Felice, at least, Kafka established a distinction between Jewish faith and the connection with some tran-
scendent entity. Thus in February 1913 he had written to her:

What is it that sustains you, the idea of Judaism or of God?
Are you aware, and this is the most important thing, of a
continuous relationship between yourself and a reassuringly

distant, if possibly infinite height or depth? He who feels this continuously has no need to roam about like a lost dog, mainly gazing around with imploring eyes; he never need yearn to step into a grave as if it were a warm sleeping bag and life a cold winter night; and when climbing the stairs to his office he never need imagine that he is careening down the well of the staircase, flickering in the uncertain night, twisting from the speed of his fall, shaking his head with impatience.[36]

In July 1922, two years before his death, Kafka reiterated in a letter to Brod his lack of connection with Judaism as religion. Regarding the relation to his father, he wrote about himself as "unloving, alienated from the Faith, so that a father cannot even expect him to say the prayers for the rest of his soul."[37] It was as definitive a statement as could be.

3

Although he was in high school at the time of the anti-Jewish violence of the late 1890s, Kafka didn't seem to pay attention to it, nor did he react to the unfolding of the Hilsner ritual murder affair that agitated Bohemia at the turn of the century. On one occasion, years later, he mentioned Hilsner and accusations of ritual murder more generally, in a letter to Milena.[38] As for the Beilis ritual murder trial of 1912–1913 in Kiev, which drew worldwide attention, it didn't leave any direct trace in Kafka's writings, although as a regular reader of *Selbstwehr* he certainly followed the detailed coverage of it. (Some commentators have attempted to prove the existence of allusions to the trial in "The Judgment," "In the Penal Colony," and *The Trial*, although evidence is scant.)[39] But Kafka's concern with antisemitism grew apace after the war, as incitement against the Jews became threatening in Eastern and Central Europe.

When, in 1920, anti-Jewish riots broke out in Prague, in the new Czechoslovak republic, Kafka reacted vehemently. "I have been spending every afternoon in the streets," he wrote to Milena in mid-November, "wallowing in anti-Semitic hate. The other day I heard someone call Jews a 'mangy race.' Isn't it natural to leave a place where one is so hated? (Zionism or national feeling isn't needed for this at all.) The heroism of staying on is nonetheless merely the heroism of cockroaches which cannot be exterminated even from the bathroom. I just looked out of the window: Mounted police, gendarmes with fixed bayonets, a screaming mob dispersing, and up here in the window the unsavory shame of living under constant protection."[40]

Throughout the letters and the diaries of these postwar years, Kafka commented upon major anti-Jewish attacks, such as the murder of the Jewish foreign minister of Germany, Walther Rathenau, in June 1922. Kafka's reaction to this event in a letter to Brod from June 30 gives the impression that for him such outbreaks of violence and murderousness were predetermined and inescapable: "The ghastly news? Are you referring to something else besides the assassination of Rathenau? It's incomprehensible that they let him live as long as they did. Two months ago a rumor of his assassination was going around in Prague. Prof. Münzer spread it—so credible was it, so consistent with the linked destinies of Jews and Germans."[41]

Kafka was aware of the major anti-Jewish publications of these years, such as the *Protocols of the Elders of Zion*, on which he commented in a letter to Felix Weltsch sent from Meran in April or May 1920. Two years later he became strongly agitated by Hans Blüher's *Secessio Judaica* and tried to persuade his new friend, a young Hungarian Jew, Robert Klopstock, to write a critical review of it. As for the milder social prejudice against Jews, such as the reaction of his table companions at the Matliary sanatorium when he told them that he was a Jew, Kafka at times described it with a whiff of amusement. Yet there is also more than a hint of bitterness when he wrote to Milena, who was married to a Jew, about an incident stemming from her own milieu: "An example [of the threats Jews perceive] is vaguely connected with you. . . . My youngest sister is supposed to marry a Czech, a Christian. When he once told a relative of yours that he intended to marry a Jewess, she said: 'Anything but that, anything rather than getting mixed up with Jews! Just think: our Milena . . .'"[42]

Kafka's stronger interest in Jewish issues since the end of 1911, especially his increased awareness of antisemitism, might have been expected to lead him toward the kind of "cultural Zionism" prevalent in Prague, from the early years of the century.[43] In contrast to Theodor Herzl's Zionism, essentially centered upon achieving political aims, the essence of cultural Zionism was bolstering the knowledge of Hebrew language and culture as a step toward the creation of a "spiritual center" in Palestine that would serve as a model for inspiring and unifying the Diaspora. While Ahad Ha'am (Asher Zwi Ginzberg) became the main figure of cultural Zionism worldwide, the Prague Zionists Hugo Bergmann, Max Brod, and Felix Weltsch were under the influence of Martin Buber's writings and lectures. Buber's impact on the Prague Zionists reached a high point in the years 1909–1910, when he delivered three lectures subsequently published as *Drei Reden über das Judentum (Three Lectures on Judaism)* in which he propounded a synthesis of spirituality and national (*völkisch*) myths; Ahad Ha'am, in contrast, remained a secularist through and through. Kafka probably attended Buber's last lecture; he certainly knew of Buber's ideas from *Selbstwehr* and from the enthusiastic reactions of his friends. Yet as we have seen, he had no great regard for Buber's performances.

Buber's main message focused upon the rebirth of a Jewish spiritual identity that would suffuse and empower the rebirth of the Jewish Volk, a spiritual identity still alive in the myths and legends of Eastern European Hasidism. Among Prague Zionists led by Brod, the corollary of such a renewed Jewish spiritual identity was pushed to extremes: it meant, for example, that Jewish authors should reject the primacy of German culture and adopt a "Jewish German" culture sui generis. The debate that had found its strongest echo in the *Kunstwart* controversy—in which German antisemites and Jewish cultural separatists found common ground in demanding a clear-cut distinction between German culture and a specific Jewish or a clearly defined "Jewish German" one with its own content and even its own mode of expression—flared up again during the war years. Brod, and with him the *Selbstwehr* group, became ever more fanatical and aggressive regarding all Jewish writers (Brod used the demeaning term *Literaten*) who went on working in German without taking into account any distinction. Brod led countless and increasingly absurd battles against all Jews in the field of German letters, except for Kafka.[44] Giuliano Baioni has thoroughly described the antics of the Prague cultural Zionists but has failed to mention that in the letter of June 1921 about the "impossibilities" facing Jews who wanted to write in German, Kafka appeared to adopt at least part of Brod's criticism without, however, siding with his program.

In that letter, Kafka wavered: on the one hand, he seemed to agree with a recent attack by Karl Kraus against Jewish authors whose German couldn't get rid of Yiddish traces (*mauscheln*), then accused Kraus of the same weakness, though he did not adopt Brod's position in favor of some Jewish-German *littérature engagée*. Finally—and this Brod couldn't know at the time—Kafka remained a Kraus devotee to the end.[45]

Notwithstanding all of Brod's efforts to prove otherwise, Kafka was no Zionist; his attitude towards Zionism was one of distant sympathy at best.[46] He described his position in a letter to Felice's friend Grete Bloch in June 1914. Speaking of himself in the third person, Kafka wrote: "Owing to circumstances as well as to his own temperament, a completely antisocial man in an indifferent state of health hard to determine at the moment, excluded from every great soul—sustaining community on account of his non-Zionist (I admire Zionism and am nauseated by it), non-practicing Judaism."[47]

And to Felice he wrote in 1916: "Should you one day feel yourself to be a Zionist (you flirted with it once, but these were mere flirtations, not a coming to terms), and subsequently realize that I am not a Zionist . . . it wouldn't worry me, nor need it worry you; Zionism is not something that separates well-meaning people."[48]

Since 1911 Kafka had become a regular reader of the Zionist periodical *Selbstwehr* (Self-defense); he even subscribed to the periodical from 1917 on.[49] He went to lectures on Zionism and, somewhat by chance, he attended part of the debates of the Eleventh Zionist Congress on the occasion of a visit to Vienna in September 1913. In October 1921 he went to see a film on life in Palestine: *Shivat Zion* (*Return to Zion*).[50] Otherwise, he avoided any further commitment. This, however, leaves two unresolved questions: What led Kafka to learn Hebrew assiduously from 1917 on? How serious were his allusions, during the last two years of his life, to leaving for Palestine?

Kafka started learning Hebrew on his own in 1917, using Moses Rath's textbook.[51] Later he studied with a number of teachers, among them his friend Friedrich Thieberger and then, daily, with the Palestine-born, native Hebrew-speaker Puah Ben-Tovim. After Ben-Tovim left Prague, Kafka went back to a textbook and again proceeded on his own. Had Kafka studied Hebrew in order to move to Palestine, he would have mentioned it.

With Puah, Kafka even attempted to read a modern Hebrew novel: Yosef Haim Brenner's *Barrenness and Failure* (*Schol*

Vekishalon). He commented about it in a letter to Brod in October 1923: "I am not enjoying the book very much as a novel. I have always had a certain awe of Brenner; I don't know exactly why. Imagination and things I have heard were mingled in my feeling about him. There has always been talk of his sadness . . . sadness in Palestine?"[52] This may have been Kafka's way of telling Brod: Your unconditional Zionism should take into account that one could also be unhappy in Palestine. Brenner was murdered in Jaffa in the May 1921 Arab riots.

In fact, notwithstanding Kafka's lack of appreciation for the quality of Brenner's novel, the study of Hebrew allowed him to read the Bible in its original text, and at the end of his life he even added some Aramaic. With Dora Diamant, he followed courses on the Bible and the Talmud at the Berlin Hochschule für die Wissenschaft des Judentums.[53] It was all food for the undernourished Jewish soul . . .

As for Kafka's sporadic remarks during the last year of his life about settling in Palestine and opening a restaurant where Dora would cook and he would be the waiter, these were of course mere fantasies, stories that Kafka was imagining like any other of his stories. He knew perfectly well that, by then, his illness precluded any such traveling or any new life in particularly difficult material conditions. One minor initiative, however, warrants a (very small) question mark.

As he was vacationing in Müritz on the Baltic Sea in July 1923, Kafka exchanged letters with Hugo Bergmann, who had returned to Palestine from a short visit to Europe, and with Bergmann's wife, Else, who was still in Germany. Kafka seems to have agreed, in principle, to accompany Else on her journey back—probably for a short stay with the Bergmanns in Jerusalem. He thus presented his trip to Müritz as a successful test run for the "greater" journey to Palestine. In fact, Bergmann did not want Kafka to come: their house was too small, he would have to sleep in the children's room, he was too ill . . .

while Else still insisted. It then became known that no additional berths were available on the ship on which she was sailing; when Else informed Kafka of the situation, later in July, his answer indicates, it seems, his real intentions.

"Dear, dear Frau Else, . . . I know that now I shall certainly not sail—how could I sail—but that along with your letter the ship virtually docks at the threshold of my room and that you are standing there asking me, and asking me as you do, which is no small thing. . . . The hope persists for later, and you are kind and do not dash it."[54] To Milena, Kafka wrote in the same vein: "In Müritz . . . I had, after all, wanted to go to Palestine in October. . . . Naturally, it would have never happened, it was a fantasy, like the fantasy of someone convinced he will never leave his bed again. If I am never going to leave my bed, why shouldn't I go at least as far as Palestine?"[55] It is probable that Kafka would have visited Palestine had he been healthier, as such a visit was very much on his mind. Whether he would have settled there is most unlikely.

Kafka was loyal to individuals, not to causes. He wasn't tied by any political or social commitment, although he never denied his Jewish identity and tried to nourish it intellectually as much as he could. But when (as Franz later mentioned in a letter to Milena) his sister Ottla decided to marry Joseph David, a non-Jewish Czech and moreover a Czech nationalist and something of an antisemite, her brother stood by her against the initial opposition of the family and Brod's explicit doubts. On February 20, 1919, Franz wrote to his sister: "That you are doing something extraordinary and doing correctly the extraordinary is also extraordinarily difficult, you know. But if you succeed to never forget the responsibility that such a difficult act entails, if you remain conscious that you are stepping out of the rank . . . and, notwithstanding this awareness, believe that you are strong enough to carry the matter to a positive end, then—to close on a bad joke—you will have done more than if you had married 10 Jews."[56]

4

What about the "Jewishness" of Kafka's fiction? Did he explicitly write on Jewish themes? Was he influenced by Jewish sources (biblical, secular, mystical)? Did he adopt some forms of Jewish religious debates (Talmudic discussions, in particular)?

The only explicitly Jewish story in Kafka's fictional work, "In Our Synagogue," probably written between the end of 1920 and autumn 1921, was discovered among the material now included in the revised German edition of his complete works. It is a minor story but one that probably expresses Kafka's view of the Judaism of his father's generation.

The story tells of an animal, "the size of a marten," that lives in the synagogue of a small community in the Tatra mountains in Slovakia. What kind of animal it is exactly, we don't know. We know, however, that it is ugly, with a triangular face, long neck, protruding teeth and brushlike coat. "Its color is a light blue-green. Nobody has yet touched its fur, so that nothing can be said about it; one could say in fact the real color of the fur is unknown, as the color we see can possibly be that of the accumulated dust and mortar of the walls caught in it; the color also looks like that of the plaster in the inside of the synagogue, except that it's slightly lighter . . ."[57] Aren't we faced with the indeterminate aspect and the uncertain "color" of Jewishness as Kafka perceived it?

We cannot know what Kafka had in mind when he wrote this "Jewish" text: there are no diary entries from the period spent at the Matliary sanatorium, where he wrote the story, and the letters he sent to Brod, Klopstock, or others during these same months do not mention "In Our Synagogue." Could it be that Kafka's uncertainty about an authentic Jewishness prodded him to write a Jewish story on the one hand but hampered him in its full scale unfolding on the other? Or, is the message of the story clear enough?

In "The Married Couple," probably written in 1922, Kafka described the distasteful social aspects of the Jewish milieu (without its Jewishness being mentioned) to which his father belonged (its single-minded business drive, its uncouth manners, and so on); in "In Our Synagogue," it is the barrenness of Jewish spiritual life that seems to be the subject: two sides of the same coin—the sorry state of Jewry in Kafka's day.

Where these spiritual blights could lead European Jewry (or Central European Jewry) is alluded to in the synagogue story: the animal "seems to be attached to nothing else but to the building itself and its personal misfortune derives from the fact that this building is a synagogue, a very crowded building at times. If one had the possibility to communicate with the animal, one could certainly comfort it with the fact that the community of our small mountain town is getting smaller from year to year and that it is already difficult for it to cover the costs of the synagogue. It cannot be excluded that in some time the synagogue will be turned into a granary or something like that and that the animal will get the rest that it now so painfully lacks."[58]

The search for Jewish themes in Kafka's major fiction is problematic. Nowadays very few interpreters would follow Max Brod in attributing a Jewish religious meaning to *The Castle*, for example. Nonetheless, we might consider "A Report to the Academy" to be a satire of assimilation (of mimicry as a supposed foundation of assimilation), "Chacals and Arabs" to be somehow related to Zionism or to Diaspora Jewry, and, possibly, in a very different mode, Kafka's final story, "Josephine the Singer, or the Mouse Folk" as an allegory for Jewish Fate. Arguably, such equivalence between a Kafka story and a specific theme, be it Jewish or not, is to turn his literary creations into allegories based on a one-to-one relation to "reality." This category of stories exists in Kafka's fiction, but none of his major texts belongs to it.

This, incidentally, leads to the obverse problem. As the main fiction offered manifold interpretations, these were often pulled toward Christianity, even recently. Thus in the foreword to Kafka's *Complete Stories*, Updike writes: "Kafka, however unmistakable the ethnic source of his 'liveliness' and alienation, avoided Jewish parochialism, and his allegories of pained awareness take upon themselves the entire European—that is to say, predominantly Christian—malaise."[59] European, maybe; human, certainly; Christian, improbably (notwithstanding the frequent use of Christian themes as metaphors.)

Some interpreters have adopted a Jewish historical-secular angle that looks plausible, albeit somewhat anachronistic. I am referring, of course, to Hannah Arendt's well-known 1944 essay "The Jew as Pariah: A Hidden Tradition," in which she quotes Gardena, the landlady of the Bridge Inn in *The Castle* telling K.: "You are not of the castle, you are not of the village, you are nothing at all."[60] When Arendt wrote the essay, the "pariah" interpretation of the Jewish condition was by far more appropriate than even she probably knew. For Kafka, K. may have been the Jew rejected by modern society, but such an identification could also have been—and more probably so in the early 1920s—only a side aspect of a more general human alienation in modern society, a relentless probing of the human predicament.

Kafka did borrow from Judaism, but in a highly idiosyncratic way. The aphorisms are, of course, heavily influenced by biblical texts and by various Rabbinic or esoteric Jewish writings (including Jewish mysticism); so is the fiction, but differently: first, at the level of narrative construction and internal discourse, where the influence of Talmudic debates is unmistakable; second, at the level of images, metaphors, symbols, and legends.

Over more than two decades, in the 1920s and 1930s, Gershom Scholem, the preeminent scholar of Jewish mysticism, shared thoughts about Kafka with his close friend the philosopher and literary critic Walter Benjamin, particularly on Kafka's relation to Judaism.[61] In a letter of August 1, 1931, Scholem mentioned to Benjamin the remarkable similarity of form in the debate between the prison chaplain and Joseph K., in the Cathedral scene of *The Trial*, to traditional exegetic debates in rabbinic literature, mainly in the Talmud. The Kafka scholar Stéphane Moses developed Scholem's remark and systematically identified these similarities. However, when it came to content, Scholem apparently overstated the influence of Jewish mysticism (Kabbalah) on Kafka. On that point Scholem's most influential student, Moshe Idel, may well have come closer to what could be ascertained: "There is little Kabbalah to be found in Kafka," Idel wrote. "Although I do not claim that he was unaware of or not influenced by Kabbalah, in my opinion his unparalleled insights into the nature of reality differ dramatically from Kabbalist ideas. Much more of Kafka is found in Scholem's own understanding of Kabbalah than is found of Kabbalah in Kafka."[62]

In 1934, on the tenth anniversary of Kafka's death, Benjamin wrote a long essay about his work.[63] But the letter he sent to Scholem in June 1938, more specifically dealing with Kafka's relation to Judaism, may be of greater significance here.[64]

According to Benjamin, Kafka was listening in (*lauschen*) on tradition, but what reached him was merely something vague. No doctrine could be learned; in Kafka's work the tradition had fallen ill. The truth that it carried was to be grasped only in its haggadic essence. (The world of *Haggadah* is that of the legends that grew around the religious doctrine—the *Halacha*.)

Kafka's genius, according to Benjamin, was to have been

the first to replace the seeking of "the Truth" in tradition for the pondering upon its transmissibility, upon its haggadic element, upon the world of legends. Kafka's work is essentially made of parables, but they are not parables "that merely lie down at the feet of the doctrine as the Haggadah lies down at the feet of the Halachah"; as they lie there, "they at times raise, as if by mistake, a huge claw against" the doctrine.

Thus, Benjamin goes on, in Kafka's work the nature of wisdom isn't discussed but rather its disintegrated remnants, which are two: rumor about the true things and madness. Madness—the creative madness referred to by Benjamin—belongs, according to him, to the animals that Kafka introduces so profusely into his fiction and to the "assistants."[65]

Whether Kafka's animals are the carriers of madness remains to be shown. The more puzzling remark is about the assistants. If the comment deals with the assistants defined as such in Kafka's fiction, then Benjamin refers essentially to *The Castle*. If, however, "assistant" is used in a wider sense, to include messengers of all kinds, Benjamin's remarks lead to a vast interpretive panorama. Messengers are numerous in Kafka's fiction: Barnabas in *The Castle*; the messenger the Emperor sends to the builders of "The Great Wall of China"; the chaplain, the painter, and even Leni in *The Trial*; and the like. But either these messengers are unable to convey the messages imparted to them, as in "The Great Wall of China"; or, like Barnabas, they convey only fragments, never in a reliable way; or, like Leni and the painter, they report rumors—no more. As for the chaplain, he speaks in riddles, riddles in which, as he tells Joseph K., a statement and its contrary do not necessarily exclude each other. In each of these examples, the message (the Truth) is unknown, and the transmission of that truth is faulty at best.

In other terms, if we transpose Benjamin's interpretation to Kafka's implicit questions about Jewishness, pondering the trickling down of tradition is the only possible answer. One should not try to define the nature of Halacha but should attempt to find one's way, every day anew, in the forest of symbols offered by the Haggadah, by those elements of the Haggadah that have come down to us. And, in Kafka's fiction, the Truth remains inaccessible and is possibly nonexistent. The messengers themselves (or the commentators) have but hazy notions regarding the messages they carry; this very uncertainty and the never-ending query that ensues are the main contributions of Kafka's Jewishness to the world he created.

In 1938 Benjamin must have known the aphorisms Kafka had collected in blue octavo notebooks, as Brod had published them in 1931.[66] He must have recognized that, at times, Kafka despaired even of the hazy messages. Couldn't it be that the messages were but imagined renditions of nonexistent texts? On December 2, 1917, Kafka noted in his diary: "They were given the choice of becoming kings or the kings' messengers. As is the way with children, they all wanted to be messengers. That is why there are only messengers, racing through the world. And, since there are no kings, calling out to each other the messages that have now become meaningless. They would gladly put an end to their miserable life, but they do not dare to do so because of their oath of loyalty."[67] Was Judaism, for Kafka—and that would be the ultimate irony—the senseless keeping of a senseless tradition, merely due to the commitment to maintain it?

3

Love, Sex, and Fantasies

AN ICONIC KAFKA photograph stares from the dust covers of several biographies and illustrates an endless number of other publications. The gaze directed at the camera is sad. The face, fully viewed from under a bowler hat set somewhat askew, is young (Kafka was twenty-five when the picture was taken); the lips do not impart even the faintest hint of a smile.

Some reproductions uncover a further part of the same photograph: next to Franz sits a beautiful dog. Kafka with a dog? How could he keep one in the rather densely populated familial apartment of those years? Only the full picture shows the dog's owner (or did the dog belong to the photographer's studio?) on the far right: the twenty-two-year-old wine-cellar hostess Julianne ("Hansi") Szokoll. We don't know much about the brief relations between Hansi and Franz, but in the picture, she seems outright joyful, while, the closer one looks, he appears ever more lost . . .[1]

From the outset, Kafka's relations with women do not look on par with his sexual fantasies. These fantasies—particularly Kafka's homoeroticism—may indeed be seen as attuned to a cultural context that spread with the turn of the century, mainly in Imperial Germany, with the growth of young male movements such as the Wandervögel and various Männerbünde (male groups).[2] That Kafka became aware of these trends is obvious, as his reading of Hans Blüher indicates later on. Nonetheless, his sexual preferences, his sexual fantasies, were quite polymorphous and thus idiosyncratic in many ways. One may reiterate, however, with a measure of confidence, that aside from the total primacy of writing, sexual issues turned into the most obsessive preoccupation of Kafka's life. But what were the issues, what were the fantasies, what was "reality"?

I

In a number of diary entries and letters, Kafka mentioned quite unflattering traits of the women he met, such as their corpulence or the stubble noticeable on their chins. Even the young women he dated were described in rather uninviting terms. Thus in mid-August 1907, he wrote to Max Brod from Triesch, where he was vacationing and flirting with two girls: "The one is called Agathe, the other Hedwig. Agathe is very ugly and so is Hedwig . . ." What followed kept to the same tone.[3] In that letter Franz also told Brod that he had *Die Opale* with him and wished he also had *Amethyste* (both were literary and pornographic periodicals, briefly published by Franz Blei).

Of course, the description of Hedwig could have been meant as a joke that Max would recognize as such. Yet in the diary, Felice Bauer herself didn't receive enthusiastic comments after Kafka met her, on August 13, 1912, at the Brods': "Bony, empty face that wore its emptiness openly. . . . Almost broken nose. Blonde, somewhat straight, unattractive hair, strong chin.

As I was taking my seat I looked at her closely for the first time, by the time I was seated I already had an unshakeable opinion."[4]

Nonetheless, Franz's flirting was insatiable. "What a muddle I have been in with girls," he wrote in June 1916. "Let me count them: there have been six since the summer. I can't resist, my tongue is fairly torn from my mouth if I don't give in and admire anyone who is admirable and love her until admiration is exhausted. With all six my guilt is almost wholly inward, though one of the six did complain of me to someone."[5] With these girls there was no question of sexual intercourse. But if we rely on the diaries, we notice that women whom Kafka pursued more seriously, like Felice Bauer and Milena Jesenska, either sexually repelled or frightened him. Two comments dealing with his relation to Felice are telling.

First this, on August 14, 1913: "Coitus as punishment for the happiness of being together. Live as ascetically as possible, more ascetically than a bachelor, that is the only possible way for me to endure marriage. But she?"[6] Only in July 1916, four years after he started wooing Felice, did they have intercourse during a short stay together in Marienbad ("With F. I have been intimate only in letters, humanly merely during the last 2 days . . .").[7]

Nonetheless, shortly after they met, a correspondence began that turned into an almost daily, explicitly tender exchange; it led to an engagement in April 1913 and to concrete plans for marriage. Felice was committed to marry Franz; he dreaded it.

In October 1913 Kafka became acquainted with Grete Bloch, a friend of Felice's who lived in Vienna, where she worked as a secretary. An exchange of letters started here, too, that very soon became increasingly seductive in tone on Franz's side. It didn't lead anywhere but shows clearly Kafka's ambivalent feelings about Felice. No wonder, then, that in July 1914 a dramatic confrontation took place at the Askanischer Hof

Hotel in Berlin, in the presence of Grete Bloch, Felice's sister Erna, and Kafka's friend Ernst Weiss, in which Felice, shaken by her fiancé's equivocations, put an end to their marriage plans.

Slowly, the correspondence started again a few months later, leading to two meetings in northern Bohemia (in each case Felice made the considerable effort of a very long railway journey under wartime conditions). During the second meeting, marriage plans were initiated once more. Then, in December 1917, a few months after Kafka had been diagnosed with tuberculosis, he definitively ended their relation in a last encounter in Prague.

On the eve of the 1914 journey to Berlin that was to turn into Kafka's "Other Trial" (in Elias Canetti's felicitous phrase),[8] Franz wrote to his sister Ottla, the only confidante in his family: "I write differently from what I speak, I speak differently from what I think, I think differently from the way I ought to think, and so it all proceeds into deepest darkness."[9]

The meeting with Julie Wohryzek in the summer of 1919 and the subsequent engagement—which led to Hermann's opposition and to Franz's "Letter"—was a short-lived affair that, in principle, was meant to lead to marriage had not the apartment where the couple was supposed to live become unavailable.

The relationship with Milena Jesenska started in the spring of 1920. Milena, a Czech journalist and translator of some of Kafka's texts, was the only passionate attachment of his life. She was a good-looking woman, much younger than Franz, and truly a free spirit. Their correspondence began as an already sick Kafka was trying to recover some health in Merano, in northern Italy. The initial contact stemmed from Milena's inquiry about some translation issues and very soon turned into an exchange intense on both sides.

Milena lived in Vienna, (badly) married to a Prague Jew,

Ernst Pollak, to the outrage of her Czech nationalist and anti-semitic family. Soon Kafka was trying to entice her to leave her husband—who didn't even bother to hide his numerous affairs—and join him, first in Merano and then possibly in Prague. Milena, arguing that she still loved Pollak notwithstanding everything, did not go along with Kafka's radical plans, but they met in Vienna for four days and then a few months later in the small Austrian-Czech border town Gmünd. By the end of the year, Franz and Milena had decided not to meet again as lovers. Whatever the deeper reasons may have been, the usual sexual obstacles certainly played a major role. I shall return to Kafka's relations with Dora Diamant in the last chapter.

Max Brod's diary entries are explicit about Franz's attitude toward Milena; on July 5, 1920, he noted: "I understand very well that for him this great passion means rescue from sex."[10] In a letter to Brod, written sometime in January or February 1921, Milena said as much:

> I understand his fear down in my deepest nerve. Further-more, it was always there, before he met me, all the time he didn't know me. I knew his fear before I knew him. I armed myself against it by understanding it. In the four days Frank [Franz] was next to me [in Vienna], he lost it. We laughed about it. I know for certain that no sanatorium will succeed in curing him. He will never be healthy, Max, as long as he has this fear. And no psychic re-enforcement can overcome this fear, because the fear prevents the re-enforcement. This fear doesn't apply just to me; it applies to everything that is shamelessly alive [*auf alles was schamlos lebt*], also to the flesh, for example. Flesh is too uncovered [*enthüllt*]; he can-not stand the sight of it . . .[11]

Milena then reproaches herself for not having had the strength to accept the kind of life she would have had in living with Kafka: "What people attribute to Frank's not being normal is actually his virtue. The women he was with were normal women and didn't know how to live any differently. . . . At the time [during Milena's relation with Kafka] I was an ordinary woman, like all women in the world, a small impulsive female [*Weibchen*]."[12]

Whether Milena understood the various aspects of Kafka's "fear" beyond what she wrote to Brod is impossible to tell. In two of his letters from August 1920, "Frank" strongly hinted at things yet unsaid. One letter was written on August 8 or 9, before Kafka's second meeting with Milena. Once more, Kafka addressed his fear of their (sexual) encounter and, in order to explain his constant inner tension between fear and longing, he evoked an old story: two meetings during his student days with an anonymous Prague shopgirl. The girl took Kafka to a hotel on the Mala Strana (Kleinseite), the old town on the castle hill. Kafka felt physically relieved, as he wrote, but was mainly content that "the whole thing had not been *more* disgusting, *more* dirty than it was."[13] After these two brief encounters, he was unable to set eyes on the girl anymore.

In that same letter, Kafka then evoked what could have been the reason for his "hostility": something—a tiny gesture, an insignificant word, to him both disgusting and dirty, but that precisely drove him with such "amazing force into this hotel, which I would have otherwise avoided with all my remaining strength."[14]

Kafka then added a few lines about desire for that small obscenity that at times shook his body and then went on:

> There were times when my body wasn't calm, when actually nothing was calm, but when I nonetheless felt no pressure whatsoever; life was good, peaceful, its only unease was hope (do you know a better one?) . . . I was always alone at such times, for as long as they lasted. Now for the first time in my life I'm encountering *such* times, when I am *not alone*. This

is why not only your physical proximity but you yourself are quieting—disquieting. This is why I don't have any longing for smut. . . . I just don't see any smut, nothing of the kind that stimulates from the outside, but there is everything that can bring forth life from within; in short, there is some of the air breathed in Paradise before the Fall. Enough of this air that there is no longing [*touha*, desire] but not enough that there isn't any "fear." So now you know. And that is also why I "feared" a night in Gmünd, but this was only the usual "fear" (which, unfortunately, is quite sufficient) I have in Prague as well; it wasn't any special fear of Gmünd.[15]

The meeting in Gmünd appears to have been particularly disastrous. In a further letter, Kafka addressed the issue as enigmatically as usual: "Just now I feel there are some things I have to tell you, unsayable things, unwritable—not to make up for something I did wrong in Gmünd, not to save something which has drowned, but to make it utterly clear to you how I am doing, so that you won't let yourself be frightened away from me. After all, that can happen with people, despite everything."[16]

Finally, in an only half-cryptic letter to Brod, in mid-April 1921, Kafka offered a more general interpretation (which could have come straight out of an introduction to psychoanalysis):

> I am not talking about the happy—in this respect happy—times of childhood, when the door was still closed, the door behind which the tribunal conferred (the father-juryman who filled all the doors has since then, a long time since, emerged). But later the fact was that the body of every other girl tempted me, but the body of the girl in whom I placed my hope (for that reason?) not at all. As long as she withheld herself from me (F) or as long as we were one (M), it was only a menace from far away, and not even so very far; but as soon as the slightest little thing happened, everything collapsed. . . . I can love only what I can place so high above me that I cannot reach it.

... But in this collapse it really was terrible; I cannot talk about that. Only this one thing: About the Hotel Imperial [where Franz and Milena stayed during his visit to Vienna] you were mistaken; what you thought was enthusiasm was funk. Only fragments of four days torn out of the night were happiness; fragments which were already locked up in the closet literally unassailable; the moaning for this achievement was happiness.[17]

But, then, Kafka could not have been surprised by a situation he knew and understood. Hadn't he written this to Brod in January 1918? "You are right in saying that the deeper realm of sexual life is closed to me; I too think so."[18]

To relieve his sexual urges, Kafka, throughout his life, either went to brothels or took prostitutes to hotels. This Brod could not deny, although he censored wherever he had a chance. Thus, for October 1, 1911, the Brod edition of the *Diaries* reads: "The day before the day before yesterday. The one, a Jewish girl with a narrow face . . ." Even a careful reader may think of a bar or a nightclub scenario.[19] The revised German edition includes a slight addition: "The day before the day before yesterday, at brothel Šuha. The one Jewish girl with a narrow face . . ."[20] Šuha was apparently one of the better-known brothels in Prague.[21] Incidentally, this entry gives Kafka the opportunity for one of his rather unflattering descriptions of women: "The landlady with the pale blonde hair drawn tight over doubtlessly disgusting pads, with the sharply slanting nose the direction of which stands in some sort of geometric relation to the sagging breasts and the stiffly held belly, complains of headaches."[22]

In an early letter to Brod, in July 1908 (the English edition mistakenly indicates September), Kafka admitted without any apparent embarrassment: "I am so urgently driven to find someone who will merely touch me in a friendly manner that yesterday I went to the hotel with a prostitute. She is too old to still be melancholy, but feels sorry, though it doesn't surprise her, that people are not so kind to prostitutes as they are to a mistress. I didn't comfort her since she didn't comfort me either."[23]

During their vacation trip to Milan, Zurich, and Paris in September 1911, Kafka and Brod visited a brothel in Milan and another one in Paris. Kafka left descriptions of both institutions and of their inmates, vivid enough to draw Brod's intervention: in Milan, a Spanish girl's "thick hair stretching from the navel to her private parts" disappeared.[24] The detailed evocation of the Paris brothel was left untouched.[25]

Before World War I, visits to brothels were encouraged as *rites de passage* for middle-class young men, as commonly as they had been part of married bourgeois men's longtime routine. Only the oft-unheeded fear of venereal disease may have prompted some second thoughts. Kafka's own attraction to prostitution has to be at least partly interpreted in its context.

In November 1913 Kafka noted: "I intentionally walk through the streets where there are whores. Walking past them excites me, the remote but nevertheless existent possibility of going with one. Is that grossness? But I know no better, and doing this seems basically innocent to me and causes me almost no regret. I want only the stout, older ones, with outmoded clothes that have, however, a certain luxuriousness because of various adornments. One woman probably knows me by now. I met her this afternoon, she was not yet in her working clothes. . . . No one would have found anything exciting in her, only me."[26] On January 23, 1922, Max Brod noted in his own diary: "At Kafka's. He moves me deeply. He told . . . of a visit to a brothel. Torture of the genitals [*Qual der Geschlechtsorgane*]."[27]

2

There was nothing that Raban, the protagonist of "Wedding Preparations in the Country," wishes more intensely than avoiding the short journey to meet his betrothed, who waits for him in the country. In this early story, which Kafka started in 1905, Raban imagines the pleasure of turning into a beetle, staying in bed, and sending his clothed body to the meeting while he is "hibernating."[28] The images, as we know, would return in life and writing.

In Kafka's fiction, women are hardly admirable. "In his great novels," the Kafka scholar Klaus Wagenbach writes, "the prostitute is virtually the only kind of woman we encounter: first in *Amerika* in the person of Brunelda . . . and even more in his two later novels, *The Trial* and *The Castle*, in the persons of Fraülein Bürstner or the servant girls Leni and Frieda, washerwomen and kept mistresses of lawyers, Castellans and officials. They are dully carnal creatures thinking only of 'present slight physical defects' and emitting a 'bitter exciting odor as of pepper.'"[29]

The women Kafka described may not have all been prostitutes, but prostitutes were those who attracted his protagonists, those who did not frighten them away from sex. Moreover, as another Kafka scholar, Ritchie Robertson, has noted regarding *Amerika*, "throughout the novel, sexually active women [who are not necessarily prostitutes] are domineering, repulsive and sometimes violent. . . . Karl's only female friend of his own age is Therese, who is eighteen but physically undeveloped. The implication is that friendship is possible only with women who do not challenge one by inviting sexual intimacy."[30] The major Kafka interpreters Reiner Stach and Elisabeth Boa argue (from opposite points of view) that Kafka's representation of women was deeply influenced by Otto Weininger's theories; it could be the case—although there is no direct indication—but isn't it more plausible that Kafka's personal sexual experiences and preferences were the main source of the female myth he created?[31]

Ultimately, in Kafka's fiction, whether they are whorish or not, *women are dangerous beings* who, in one way or another, can lead the male protagonist astray. In *The Trial*, Fräulein Bürstner, Joseph K.'s neighbor, whom he kisses so passionately at the beginning of the novel, reappears at a crucial moment, during the final scene.

In the dark of night, Joseph K., firmly held by two men, is led, along the deserted city streets, toward the execution site. At some point, K., who has nothing to lose anymore, decides to use his last strength to resist: not to walk on. "And then," the text continues, "before them Fräulein Bürstner appeared. . . . It was not quite certain that it was she, but the resemblance was close enough. Whether it was Fräulein Bürstner or not, however, did not matter to K.; the important thing was that he suddenly realized the futility of resistance. . . . He set himself in motion, and the relief his warders felt was transmitted to some extent even to himself. They suffered him now to lead the way, and he followed the direction taken by the girl ahead of him, not that he wanted to overtake her or to keep her in sight as long as possible, but only that he might not forget the lesson she had brought into his mind." The lesson seems in fact unrelated to the young woman's presence, and soon she turns into a side street, "but by this time K. could do without her and submitted himself to the guidance of his escort."[32]

Among all possible interpretations of this enigmatic segment, in which the appearance of the young woman persuades K. not to resist but to follow her (on his way to death), one of the most immediate associations is to the final lines of Goethe's second book of *Faust*, where, as Faust is dying, the "mystical choir" proclaims: "The Eternal Feminine / Pulls us upward." It might be understood as a hidden message of redemption, negating the explicit significance of Joseph K.'s death "as a dog." It might, more probably, be a heavily ironic take on Goethe's salvation pronouncement. Here, the "Eternal Feminine" is represented not by the heavenly Virgin Mary or the pure and saintly Margarethe but by a young lady of questionable virtue who may be unaware of Joseph K.'s following her and who abruptly turns into a side street. Here, the "eternal feminine" leads to perdition.

3

Throughout the years, Kafka hinted at erotic feelings for a few male friends (Oskar Pollak, Franz Werfel, Yitzhak Löwy, Robert Klopstock), but that impulse certainly did not stop him from wooing women. His own confusion did confuse interpreters less informed and less vigilant than Brod. The discrepancies between Kafka's diaries, letters, and other texts as emended by Brod and the new German standard edition highlight those passages that appeared problematic to the censor's eye. At times Brod was just prudish, as when he deleted Kafka's November 28, 1911, entry about the painter Alfred Kubin's lovemaking technique as narrated by a chance acquaintance, a Herr Pachinger from Linz.[33] Regarding another elision made on the first page of the "Travel Diary," one wonders whether it was prompted by prudishness or by the suspicion of a homosexual allusion. Kafka describes his trip to Reichenberg in northern Bohemia, in January 1911. Opposite him in the train compartment sits a rather unsavory character whom Kafka qualifies as a "windbag." He mentions his travel mate's repelling way of eating and of disposing of the trash, completing the portrait rather bluntly: "The apparently big member creates a bulge in his pants."[34]

In his reminiscences, Hugo Hecht, a schoolmate throughout Kafka's entire twelve years of elementary and high school, mentions the absence of any sweetheart during his friend's adolescence: "For Kafka, love didn't come into question at that time, as sexually he was still a child. He was simply not yet mature and would not be so when he got engaged for the first time . . ."[35] It may also mean that Kafka was otherwise interested.

Homoerotic allusions appear in Franz Kafka's earliest known close friendship, during his senior high school and early university years: the bond with Oskar Pollak. Whether Pollak felt the same way about Kafka we do not know, as we don't have his letters (Pollak, who became a distinguished art historian, was killed in 1915 on the Italian front). In a 1901 letter, Franz mentions "jealousy" and ends the letter with a reference to Oskar's relation with a girl: "Wouldn't that separate us? Isn't it strange? Are we enemies? I am very fond of you [*Ich habe Dich sehr lieb*]."[36] In 1902 Kafka sent Pollak a very short "tale," "Shamefaced Lanky and Impure at Heart," that carries more than a whiff of homoeroticism. Whatever form the attraction may have taken, after the friendship between Kafka and Pollak waned, Franz started dating girls, composing at least one erotic poem in free verse about women and becoming interested in semipornographic periodicals.

From early on, Kafka had been an admirer of a younger Prague Jewish writer, Franz Werfel. He knew Werfel and admired his poems and plays, as well as his looks. In February 1913 Kafka wrote to Felice: "Werfel read to me some new poems. . . . And the young man has grown handsome and reads with such ferocity. . . . His passion seems to set fire to his heavy body, the great chest, the round cheeks; and when reading aloud he looks as if he were about to tear himself to pieces."[37]

"Today in the coffee-house with Werfel," Kafka wrote in April 1914. "How he looked from the distance, seated at the coffee table. Stooped, half reclining even in the wooden chair, the beautiful profile of his face pressed against his chest. . . . His dangling glasses make it easier to trace the delicate outlines of his face."[38] Later again, in mid-November 1917, Kafka wrote to Brod about a dream, the ambiguity of which he himself commented on: "If I go on to say that in a recent dream I gave Werfel a kiss, I stumble right into the middle of Blüher's book. But more of that later. The book upset me [*es hat mich aufgeregt*, "the book excited me"]; I had to put it aside for two days . . ."[39] Blüher, a leading figure in the German youth movement, wrote about male erotic bonding in his 1917 work *The Role of Eroticism in Male Society.*

In January 1912 Kafka had noted in his diary: "I am supposed to pose in the nude for the artist [Ernst] Ascher, as a model for a St Sebastian."[40] In July of that year, while at the Jungborn nudist sanatorium, he wrote: "I modeled for Dr. Schiller. Without bathing trunks. An exhibitionist experience."[41]

After his youthful erotic feelings for Oskar Pollak and while harboring a subdued admiration for Werfel, Kafka appears to have been particularly attracted to Yitzhak Löwy and Robert Klopstock. Regarding Löwy, with whom Kafka spent long hours almost daily in 1911, there are a few words in the diary—which Brod censored, of course—about their visit to the National Theater: "Löwy told me about his gonorrhea; after that my hair touched his as I leant toward his head; I got frightened because of the possibility of lice."[42]

Robert Klopstock was a young Hungarian Jew whom Kafka befriended at the Matliary sanatorium in late 1920 or early 1921. A medical student, he hoped to move to Prague. In April 1921 Kafka sent a letter to Brod to introduce his new friend and explore whether Brod could suggest any source of financial help: "He [Klopstock] shows no outward signs of his illness. He is a tall, strong, broad, red-cheeked, blond fellow; when dressed he is almost too heavy. . . . Since I have introduced him somewhat by his appearance (in bed, in nightshirt with tousled hair, he has a boyish face like an engraving from Hoffmann's children's stories, earnest and tense, yet also dreamy—he is actually good-looking that way)—now that I have introduced him, I want to ask two things in his behalf."[43]

A few months later, back in Prague, Kafka wrote to Klopstock, who was still in Matliary:

> Dear Robert, Please don't be angry or, what is much the same, don't be so disturbed. I am disturbed too, but in another fashion. The situation is clear, the gods are playing with us both, but different gods for you and for me and we must exert all our human energies to equalize it. I cannot say much about the main thing, for this is, even for you, locked within the darkness of the breast. I imagine it lies there beside the disease, on the same bed. Thursday or Friday I will be alone again [Löwy was visiting] and then I may perhaps write to you about it, though even then not thoroughly, for there is no human being, myself included, who could deal with it thoroughly . . .[44]

In January 1922 Kafka, for no apparent reason, mentioned his uncle Rudolf, his mother's half-brother, in his diary. Rudolf had converted to Catholicism, and whether for that reason or because Rudolf himself shied away from the Kafkas, there were no relations between him and Franz's family. Franz established a thorough comparison of himself with his by then deceased uncle; at one point he ventured a question that looks innocuous or even meaningless in the English translation but is explicit in the original and in the French rendition. The English translation reads as follows: "Whether he [Rudolf] had to contend (inwardly) with women, I do not know, a story about him [the English translation mistakenly reads "by him"] that I heard would indicate as much; when I was a child, moreover, they spoke of something of the sort."[45]

To *contend inwardly with women* makes no sense. The German original is clearer: *Ob er um Frauen (mit sich) gekämpft hat, weiss ich nicht:* "Whether he fought for women (*against himself*),

I do not know." Marthe Robert's French translation renders the meaning of the sentence most unambiguously: "J'ignore s'il a lutté (*contre lui-même*) pour la possession des femmes."[46] The implicit comparison is obvious: Kafka does not know whether his uncle, like he himself, had to struggle to have relations with women against his inner inclinations. The additional part of the excerpt seems to indicate that there was talk in the family about Rudolf's homosexuality.

Kafka's sexual fantasies were not directed at adults only. Thus in the summer of 1912, after a brief journey with Brod to Leipzig and Weimar, Kafka arrived at the Jungborn nudist sanatorium in the Harz. Under the date of July 9, 1912, the English translation of the censored diary carries the following sentence: "Two handsome Swedish boys with long legs."[47] The German original elaborates: "2 handsome Swedish boys with long legs, that are so shaped and tight that the best way to get at them would be with the tongue [*2 schöne schwedische Jungen mit langen Beinen, die so geformt und gespannt sind, dass man nur mit der Zunge richtig an ihnen hinfahren konnte*]."[48]

The diary entry of February 2, 1922, mentioned in the introduction, is emblematic in several ways: "Struggle on the road to Tannenstein in the morning, struggle while watching the ski-jumping contest. Happy little B., in all his innocence somehow shadowed by my ghosts, at least in my eyes[, specially his outstretched leg in its gray rolled-up sock], his aimless wandering glance, his aimless talk. In this connection it occurs to me — but this is already forced — that towards evening he wanted to go home with me."[49] The passage indicates that Kafka had met B. before the day of the competition; otherwise why would there have been struggle "on the road to [the] Tannenstein"? More than such an indirect allusion, we do not know, although the two entries that follow under the same date both mention "the struggle"; the second entry reads: "The Negative having been in all probability greatly strengthened by 'the struggle,' a decision between insanity and security is imminent."[50] Does it mean: between the "insanity" of pursuing relations with B. or the "security" of avoiding him?

The company of little girls seems to have been as welcome as that of young boys. One is reminded of Lewis Carroll, of course (not least by the emended diary pages); both cases bear a measure of ambiguity.[51] In July 1912, during some festivity in Stapelburg (near Jungborn), Kafka took six little girls he had just met on the street, ages six to thirteen, to a merry-go-round: they all sat pressed together in the same carriage, one of the girls on Kafka's knees. He was ready for more, but the girls decided against it.[52]

The case of "little Lena" is the only explicit indication of physical arousal by a child. "With Felix in Rostock"—actually Rostok, near Prague—Kafka noted on July 23, 1913. "The bursting sexuality of the women. Their natural impurity. The flirtation, senseless for me, with little Lena. . . . The life on the small terrace. How I coldly took the little girl on my lap, not at all unhappy about the coolness." Here the English translation ends; the original (and the French translation) includes one further sentence: "The ascent in the silent valley."[53]

Brod and the editors of the American translation had no problem, though, with a diary entry of November 11, 1911: "The girls, tightly wrapped up in their work aprons, especially behind. One at Löwy and Winterberg [a wood warehouse] this morning whose apron flaps, which closed only on her behind, did not tie together as they usually do, but instead closed over each other so that she was wrapped up like a child in swaddling clothes. Sensual impression like that which, even unconsciously, I always had of children in swaddling clothes who are so squeezed in their wrappings and beds and so laced with ribbons, quite as though to satisfy one's lust."[54]

4

Allusions to homoeroticism are generally more open in Kafka's fiction than in his nonfictional writings. In one of Kafka's earliest stories, "Description of a Struggle," the narrator and an acquaintance are discussing love on a hill above Prague, in the depth of night. "'You are incapable of loving,' the acquaintance shouted to the narrator."

> "Only fear excites you. Just take a look at my chest." Where-upon he quickly opened his overcoat and waistcoat and his shirt. His chest was indeed broad and beautiful. . . . Then, with a limp, distorted mouth, I got up, stepped onto the lawn behind the bench . . . and whispered into my acquaintance's ear: "I'm engaged, I confess it."
>
> My acquaintance wasn't surprised that I got up. "You're engaged?" He sat there really quite exhausted, supported only by the back of the bench. Then he took off his hat and I saw his hair which, scented and beautifully combed, set off the round head on a fleshy neck in a sharp curving line, as was the fashion that winter. . . . My acquaintance mopped his brow with a batiste handkerchief. "Please put your hand on my forehead," he said. "I beg you." When I didn't do so, he folded his hands. . . . Then, without further ado, my acquain-tance pulled a knife out of his pocket, opened it thoughtfully, and then, as though he were playing, he plunged it into his left upper arm, and didn't withdraw it. Blood promptly began to flow. His round cheeks grew pale. I pulled out the knife, cut up the sleeve of his overcoat and jacket, tore his shirt sleeve open. . . . I sucked a little at the deep wound. . . . "My dear, dear friend," said I, "you've wounded yourself for my sake."[55]

The English translation of Kafka's story does not include version B of "Description of a Struggle," and this version B does not refer to the wound; it is, however, far more explicit re-garding the relationship between the narrator and his acquain-tance. "'You see then,' I said. At that moment, he pushed my hands aside with a jolt, I fell with my mouth on his mouth and immediately received a kiss" [*"Na siehst Du?" Sagte Ich. Da schob er mit einem Ruck meine Hände zur Seite, ich fiel mit dem Mund auf seinen Mund und bekam sofort einen Kuss.*][56]

Mark Anderson, who refers only to version A, stresses the homoerotic sequence triggered by the narrator's confession that he is engaged. According to his comment, this brief sequence immediately leads from the "reality" of the worldly to "an unmistakable metaphysical anxiety."[57] Indeed, in Kafka's texts metaphysical anxiety is never far from reality, in this story as in most others.

While there may be elements of expressionist mannerism in "Description of a Struggle," nothing of the kind can be found in the oft quoted night scene in *The Castle*, where K. falls asleep next to secretary Bürgel, a castle official, in Bürgel's bed. It's night and K. has wandered into the castle officials' section of the Gentlemen's Inn, where, by chance, he enters Bürgel's room and soon, exhausted by a day full of tension, sits on Bürgel's bed. Instead of chasing him away, Bürgel welcomes K. and addresses him enthusiastically in what will become an endless monologue. "Bürgel's eyes," the Kafka scholar Heinz Politzer has noted,

> are now resting on him with the same feverish longing with which K. has contemplated the Castle for six long days. A mysterious union between official and applicant is under way, an embrace both actual and metaphysical in nature. Bürgel's pronouncement [in welcoming K.] has acquired a hymnlike quality, which reveals a distinctly erotic coloration. The applicant's presence in his room invites him, as he says, "to penetrate into his poor life. . . . This invitation in the silent night is beguiling." Although Bürgel retains enough official decorum at the climax of this night scene to classify its mystery strictly as "misuses of official power," he is carried away by passion to such an extent that he is able to cry: "Never-

theless, we are happy. How suicidal happiness can be." This is the language of love.[58]

The love night unfolds in several sequences. While Bürgel goes on speaking, K., defeated by fatigue, falls asleep, still sitting on the bed. He dreams of a victory celebration in which he is the honored hero. The battle is replayed: "A secretary, naked, very like the statue of a Greek god, was being hard pressed by K. in battle. That was quite comical, and in his sleep K. smiled gently at the way the secretary was being constantly startled out of his proud posture by K.'s advances and quickly had to use his raised arm and clenched fist to cover up his exposed parts, but he was not yet quick enough. The battle did not last long, for step by step, and very big steps they were too, K. advanced. Was this even a battle? There was no real obstacle, only every so often a few squeaks from the secretary. This Greek god squeaked like a girl being tickled."[59]

K. wakes briefly and "at the sight" of Bürgel's bare chest, a thought from the dream comes to him: "There is your Greek god! So pull him out of the sack!"[60] As Bürgel drones on, K. falls asleep again, deeply and, this time, without any dreams. "His head, which initially had rested on his left arm up on the bedpost, had slid off while he slept and now hung freely, sinking slowly; the support from the arm above no longer sufficed, K. involuntarily found a new hold by bracing his right hand against the blanket, thereby accidentally grasping Bürgel's foot, which stuck up under the blanket."[61]

Possibly one of the most explicit homoerotic texts in Kafka's fiction is also one of his shortest parables about "crime" and "punishment": "The Bridge." The narrator is a small mountain bridge, spanned over a ravine and an icy stream. Nobody crosses the bridge for a very long time, until one day . . .

> He came, he tapped me with the iron point of his stick, then he lifted my coattails with it and put them in order upon me.

He plunged the point of his stick into my bushy hair and let it lie there for a long time, forgetting me no doubt while he wildly gazed around him. But then . . . he jumped with both feet on the middle of my body. I shuddered with wild pain, not knowing what was happening. Who was it? A child? A dream? A wayfarer? A suicide? A tempter? A destroyer? And I turned around so as to see him. A bridge to turn around! I had not yet turned quite around when I already began to fall, I fell and in a moment I was torn and transpierced by the sharp rocks which had always gazed up at me so peacefully from the rushing water.[62]

Some texts are more equivocal. Thus in "The Warden of the Tomb," for example, the warden describes his nightly fight against ghosts led by the Duke: "I rush out of the door, around the house, and promptly run into the Duke and there we are, locked in combat. . . . Now and again he lifts me up in the air and then I fight up there, too. All his comrades stand around in a circle and make fun of me. One, for instance, cuts open my trousers behind and they all play with the tail of my shirt while I am fighting."[63]

And there is the mysterious story of Hans and Amalia, included in a diary entry on April 20, 1916. "Hans and Amalia, the butcher's two children were playing marbles near the wall of a big warehouse . . . which extended a great distance along the riverbank . . ." Suddenly a face appears close to them at one of the "heavily barred windows." "It seemed to be a man and he said, 'come in children, come in. Have you ever seen a warehouse?'"

The story that then unfolds describes the enticements of the man, and the initially eager, then increasingly hesitant, response of the children. The man on the inside moves toward the front door and shows them the way by knocking at the windowpanes. As they all reach the front of the building, the man opens several doors one after the other. "The last door finally opened inward, the children lay down on the ground to peer inside, and there in the gloom was the man's face. 'The doors are open, come along! Be quick though, quick!' With his arm he pushed all the doors against the wall."

Amalia hides now behind Hans but, unable to withstand her curiosity, nonetheless goads her brother toward the entrance. The man wants—or so it seems—to get Amalia alone, but she insists that Hans must come too.

> "Of course," the stranger said and, lunging forward with the upper part of his body, grabbed Hans, who was taken completely unawares, by the hands so that he tumbled down at once, and with all his strength the man pulled him into the hold. "This way in, my dear Hans," he said and dragged the struggling, screaming boy inside, heedless of the fact that one of Hans's sleeves was being torn to shreds on the sharp edges of the doors. "Mali," Hans cried out—his feet had already vanished within the hole, it went so quickly despite all the resistance he put up—"Mali, get father, get father, I can't get out, he is pulling me so hard!" But Mali, completely disconcerted by the stranger's brutal onslaught—and with some feeling of guilt besides . . . though in the final analysis also quite curious, as she had been from the very beginning—did not run away but held on to Hans's feet and let . . .[64]

There Kafka's story ends.

It is highly improbable that Kafka ever considered the possibility of homosexual relations. Yet as Mark Anderson has stressed, the issue has to be set in different terms. Referring to Brod's presentation of Kafka (which contradicts the *Diaries* and his personal observations), Anderson writes: "Kafka's disgust with (hetero-) sexual relations fits conveniently into this image: a saint who eschews all earthly temptation for the sake of his writing. But disgust is precisely what is lacking in Kafka's characterization of desire between men. Though it may provoke a variety of emotional responses ranging from simple affirmation and childlike fascination to near-sublime moments of terror and pain, homosexual desire does not trigger the same order of emotional denial that the mere thought of marriage and heterosexual relations induced."[65]

Possibly no less significant is the "gender-neutral" way in which Kafka often describes women, using, for example, "*Brust* (chest) rather than the female-specific *Busen* or *Brüste* (breasts)." Dagmar Lorenz, who makes that point, expands it by quoting from *Amerika*, in which Karl Rossmann finds himself in the exiguous Stoker's cabin: "'Just lie down on the bed, you'll have more room,' said the man [the Stoker]. Karl crawled inside as best as he could and laughed out loud at his forlorn attempt to swing himself over. . . . 'Just stay,' the man said, pushing against his chest quite roughly with one of his hands so that he fell back into the bed." "The roughness of the older man," Lorenz adds, "the enforced compliance of the younger, simulate male and female patterns in an all-male environment."[66]

5

Kafka did not hide his sadomasochistic fantasies, which have been recognized by his biographers.[67] We have seen that Gregor, the huge bug of *The Metamorphosis*, tried to save the picture of *Venus in Furs* from the hands of mother and sister. This was but the overture to a long series of texts.

"A vulture was hacking at my feet. It had already torn my boots and stockings to shreds, now it was hacking at the feet themselves. Again and again it struck at them, then circled several times restlessly around me, then returned to continue its work." This strangest of openings to Franz Kafka's short story "The Vulture" takes up his ever-present obsession with torture. In one of his last letters to Milena he states emphatically: "Yes, torturing is extremely important to me, I am preoccupied with nothing but being tortured or torturing. . . . The stupidity inherent in this (realization of stupidity doesn't help) I once expressed as follows: 'The animal wrenches the whip from the master and whips itself so as to become master, and doesn't realize that it's only a fantasy caused by a new knot in the master's thong.'"[68]

The animal in Kafka's letter does not recognize the pleasure that drives it, the pleasure caused by the new knot. As for the narrator attacked by the vulture, did he expect the ecstasy of the end? "It [the vulture] took wing, leaned far back to gain impetus, and then like a javelin thrower, thrust its beak through my mouth, deep into me. Falling back, I was relieved to feel him drowning irretrievably in my blood, which was filling every depth, flooding every shore."[69]

Clearly, Kafka enjoys describing the most elaborate torture scenes: "To be pulled in through the ground-floor window of a house," Kafka noted in his diary on July 21, 1913, "by a rope tied around one's neck and to be yanked up, bloody and ragged, through all the ceilings, furniture, walls, and attics, without consideration, as if by a person who is paying no attention, until the empty noose, dropping the last fragments of me when it breaks through the roof tiles, is seen on the roof."[70] A few weeks beforehand, on May 4, he had written: "Always the image of a pork butcher's broad knife that quickly and with mechanical regularity chops into me from the side and cuts off very thin slices which fly off almost like shavings because of the speed of the action."[71] Most of Kafka's torture scenes would demand further interpretation. Here, the "pork butcher's broad knife" points to the "unclean" nature of the victim, like *Ungeziefer* in *The Metamorphosis*.

In other texts, Kafka displays the cool clinical distance of the anatomist or of the forensic expert. On September 16, 1915, he noted: "Between throat and chin would be the most rewarding place to stab. Lift the chin and stick the knife into the tensed muscles. But this spot is probably rewarding only in one's imagination. You expect to see a magnificent gush of blood and a network of sinews and little bones like you find in the leg of a roast turkey."[72]

Nowhere in Kafka's descriptions of torture is there space between the executioner and the hapless or consenting (even complicit) victim. This absence of space lifts a veil that Kafka had never fully drawn: the tortured and the torturer are often either one and the same individual or two individuals linked by a pact of sadomasochistic complicity. "This morning," Kafka noted in his diary on November 2, 1911, "For the first time in a long time, the joy again of imagining a knife twisted in my heart."[73] The vagaries of translation led to the use of different English words in the diary entry and in the last lines of *The Trial*, but in the original German the "twisting" of the knife is the same in both texts and described by the same verb: *drehen*.

"In the Penal Colony" offers complete and explicit identity between executioner and victim, but the self-immolation of the officer does not lead to either revelation or redemption, as supposedly had been the case for victims of the torture machine in times past: "It [the officer's face] was as it had been in life; no sign was visible of the promised redemption. What the others had found in the machine the officer had not found; the lips were firmly pressed together, the eyes were open, with the same expression as in life, the look was calm and convinced, through the forehead went the point of the great iron spike."[74]

Whether leading to ecstasy or redemption, or whether merely confirming preestablished beliefs, self-immolation never appears to usher an ultimate reaction of panicky retreat. It remains throughout Kafka's world an obsessively narrated story and a no less obsessively used metaphor: "My mind is daily prey to fantasies," he wrote to Brod, on April 3, 1913, "for example that I lie stretched out on the floor, sliced up like a roast, and with my hand am slowly pushing a slice of the meat toward a dog in the corner."[75]

In some sequences, as we have seen, the narrator imagines torturing himself and craves it; in other ones, however, the narrator—or, quite explicitly, Kafka himself—describes the torture he imagines inflicting upon others (mostly, but not exclusively, on animals).

"Just whip the horse properly!" Kafka writes down in his diary on July 21, 1913. "Dig the spurs into him slowly, then pull them out with a jerk, but now let them bite into the flesh with all your strength."[76] A year later or so, the narrator in "Memoirs of the Kalda Railway"—a story inserted in the diaries under August 15, 1914—tells how he dealt with some of the rats he caught in his hut: "During the first days, when I was eagerly taking in everything, I spitted one of these rats on the point of my knife and held it before me at eye level against the wall. . . . Hanging against the wall in front of me in its final agony, it rigidly stretched out its claws in what seemed to be an unnatural way; they were like small hands reaching out to you."[77]

Kafka also dreams about torture. On April 20, 1916, he writes down in his diary: "A dream: Two groups of men were fighting each other. The group to which I belonged had captured one of our opponents, a gigantic naked man. Five of us clung to him. . . . An oven stood nearby whose extraordinarily large cast-iron door was red-hot, we dragged the man to it, held one of his feet close to the oven until the foot began to smoke, pulled it back again until it stopped smoking, then thrust it close to the door again. We monotonously kept this up until I awoke, not only in cold sweat but with my teeth actually chattering."[78]

In September 1920, Kafka had sent to Milena an illustration of his torturing inventiveness: "So that you can see something of my 'occupations,' I am enclosing a drawing. These are four poles, through the two middle ones are driven rods to which the hands of the 'delinquent' are fastened; through the two outer poles rods are driven for the feet. After the man has been bound in this way the rods are drawn slowly outwards until the man is torn apart in the middle. Against the post leans the inventor who, with crossed arms and legs, is giving himself great airs, as though the whole thing were his original invention, whereas he has only copied the butcher who stretches the disemboweled pig in his shop-front."[79]

Although the closest representation of a dominatrix appears in *The Castle* in the person of the female schoolteacher, it is in *The Trial* that we find scenes of sadism and an extraordinarily vivid evocation of sadomasochism. In a demonstration of mental sadism, the lawyer Huld and his servant-mistress-nurse Leni wantonly humiliate the lawyer's elderly client, the manufacturer Block: "The client ceased to be a client and became the lawyer's dog. If the lawyer were to order this man to crawl under the bed [Huld lies in bed while Block kneels close to it] as if into a kennel and bark there, he would gladly obey the order."[80] Thus thinks Joseph K., who witnesses the scene.

Block is terrified to hear from Huld, after years of waiting, that, according to a judge, the tradesman's case has not even begun: "In embarrassment Block sat plucking at the hair of the fur rug lying before the bed; his terror of the Judge's utterance was so great that it overcame for a while his subjection to the lawyer and he was thinking only of himself, turning the Judge's words round and surveying them from all sides. 'Block,' said Leni in a tone of warning, catching him by the collar and jerking him upward a little, 'leave the rug alone and listen to the lawyer.'"[81]

As for the sadomasochistic scene that takes place in the bank where Joseph K. works, it is so realistic that it could come straight out of a gay leather bar. As K. is walking along a corridor, he hears sighs behind the door of what should be a lumber room. He tears the door open and sees three men: "the Whipper" and two others—his former warders—about to be whipped. The Whipper "was sheathed in a sort of dark leather garment which left his throat and a good deal of his chest and the whole of his arms bare."[82] The two former warders are being punished because K. has complained about them during his first appearance in court: they had gobbled his breakfast and stolen some of his underwear. He tries to intercede for them, but in vain. "'Can the birch-rod cause such terrible pain?' asked K., examining the switch, which the man [the Whipper] waved to and fro in front of him. 'We'll have to take off all our clothes first,' said Willem [one of the former warders]. 'Ah, I see,' said K., and he looked more attentively at the Whipper, who was tanned like a sailor and had a brutal, healthy face."[83]

K. suddenly closes the door as the shriek of one of the warders, hit by the whip, draws the clerks' attention; K. explains the shriek away. As he ponders the scene he comes up with a weird idea (in which one cannot but recognize Kafka's masochistic cravings): "If a sacrifice had been needed, it would almost have been simpler to take off his own clothes and offer himself to the Whipper as a substitute for the warders."[84]

When, the next day, K., passes by the lumber room, he opens the door again and, again, discovers the same scene. "At once K. slammed the door shut and then beat on it with his fists, as if that would shut it more securely."[85] The door of the lumber room will become the door of the pigsty in "A Country Doctor" and the Whipper will turn into the groom; there is one difference, however: in the short story, the whip is in the doctor's hand and he doesn't use it.

"The dream about the sick woman," Kafka wrote sometime at the end of 1917, "whom I take care of in the ambulance and who, on my demand, beats me."[86]

On February 10, 1922, shortly after his arrival in Spindelmühle, Kafka inscribed a quasi-mystical entry in his diary: "Great, tall commander-in-chief, leader of multitudes, lead the despairing through the mountain passes no one else can find beneath the snow. And who is it that gives you your strength? He who gives you your clear vision." A fragment immediately follows that strengthens the impact of the opening lines: "The commander-in-chief stood at the window of the ruined hut and looked outside with wide, unblinking eyes at the column of troops marching by in the snow under the pale moonlight. Now and then it seemed to him that a soldier out of ranks would stop by the window, press his face against the pane, look at him for a moment, and then go on. . . . Each time that the man walked away he would straighten the straps of his pack, shrug his shoulders, and get back into step with the mass of troops marching by as always in the background."[87] The oneiric mode of the opening invocation and the overall urgency expressed in the entry convey a feeling of deep need for a leader-savior.

As usual, the text is sufficiently opaque to leave us guessing. The first lines of the entry, inscribed just before the appeal to the "Great, tall commander-in-chief," without any separation between the two parts, are in fact incomprehensible in their current English translation. "New attack by G." In the German original, the mysterious and aggressive "G." means *Geschlecht*, sex. Thus the first part of the entry should read as follows: "Attacked again by sex. It is clearer than ever that attacked from right and left by overwhelming enemies, I cannot escape either to the right or to the left; only forwards, hungry beast, leads the way to food that you can eat, to air that you can breathe, to a free life be it beyond life."[88] The invocation to the "great, tall commander-in-chief" immediately follows.

Part II

"The Reward for Serving the Devil"

4

Night Journey

ON SEPTEMBER 25, 1917, half a year or so after writing "A Country Doctor" and a few weeks after being diagnosed with a lung infection (soon to be identified as tuberculosis), Kafka noted in his diary: "I can still have passing satisfaction from works like 'A Country Doctor,' provided I can still write such things at all (very improbable). But happiness only if I can raise the world into the pure, the true and the immutable."[1]

What did the second sentence mean? How did Kafka imagine "the pure, the true and the immutable"? Did he consider "A Country Doctor," the story that gave him satisfaction, as partaking of that effort toward a radical transformation? Enigmatic as usual, Kafka left us with a story and a riddle. In fact, the story itself remains a riddle, notwithstanding all exegesis. Yet this short text, one of Kafka's most accomplished creations, evokes indirectly some of the major issues to which he kept returning: a shameful absence of feelings and moral responsibility, a confused and confusing sexuality, the evasiveness of truth and, mainly, the Evil in the world and of the world.

I

On a wintry night, an old country doctor has been called to a village ten miles away, where a seriously ill patient needs his help. He is waiting, "muffled in furs," his medical bag in hand, his carriage ready; during this same night, his exhausted horse has died. Rosa, the maid, is running around in the village to borrow a horse. "It was hopeless, I knew it, and I stood there forlornly, with the snow gathering more and more thickly upon me, more and more unable to move. In the gateway the girl appeared, alone, and waved the lantern; of course, who would lend a horse at this time for such a journey?"[2] The contrast between the immobility of the old man standing in the courtyard as the snow is accumulating around him and his young maid "running around the village" is stark, but he does not seem to notice it. Very soon, he will bitterly regret having been so oblivious of her presence.

In despair, the doctor kicks at the door of a long abandoned pigsty. In quick succession, a groom, showing an "open blue-eyed face," and two magnificent horses crawl out. The groom starts harnessing, the maid is told to give him a hand, but as she stands near him, he grabs her and bites her on the cheek, leaving the imprint of two rows of teeth. The groom "marked" her; she now belongs to him, as a mark burned into the ears of cattle identifies their owner. Furious, the doctor threatens the groom with the whip, yet soon gives up and settles in the carriage. Ordered to come along, the groom refuses, and before the doctor can react, on the groom's signal, the horses and the carriage tear off. The doctor merely hears the door of his house "splitting and bursting as the groom charged at it," in pursuit of Rosa the maid, fleeing in terror "with a justified presentiment that her fate was inescapable."[3]

The pigsty, like the lumber room in *The Trial*, has often been identified as the Freudian unconscious, replete with libidinal drives. And indeed, the doctor has long neglected that pigsty and deems it "uninhabited." "You never know what you are going to find in your house," the maid pointedly comments, showing that she had some intuition of matters the doctor does not perceive. A tight series of blunt sexual metaphors follows, starting with the two horses, "enormous creatures with powerful flanks . . . [that] by sheer strength of their buttocks squeezed out through the door hole which they filled entirely. But at once they were standing up, their legs long and their bodies steaming thickly."[4] Then, the groom's unfettered sexual violence erupts. Thus from the pigsty emerge the doctor's repressed sexual urges, embodied by the groom.

There is a moment of moral choice in this first part of the story, when the doctor can save himself from the fate that will soon engulf him. As the groom attacks the maid, the doctor threatens him with the whip but quickly relents, knowing full well that at that very instant the groom has won. The moral imperative is clear: defend the victim of wanton sexual violence, use the whip, stay with the maid to protect her. But the doctor betrays the maid under the implicit pretext of professional duty. That decisive moment indicates the breakdown of all ego defenses overcome by the violent rise of libido.

In no time, the doctor's carriage stops in front of the patient's farmyard. In brief, staccato sentences Kafka describes the family, the room, the young patient who "throws his arms around [the doctor's] neck" and whispers to him: "Doctor, let me die." After a perfunctory examination, the doctor concludes that nothing is wrong with the boy and, while the ghostly horses push the windows open from the outside, insert their heads into the room, and eye the patient, he ponders how to leave without causing too much of an uproar. "I had once more been called out needlessly, I was used to that, the whole district made my

life a torment with my night bell, but that I should have to sacrifice Rosa this time as well, the pretty girl who had lived in my
house for years almost without my noticing her—that sacrifice
was too much to ask . . ."[5]

However, what appears as the end of the visit turns out to
be its real beginning. The boy's tearful mother and sister entice
the doctor to have another look, and "this time," he tells us, "I
discovered that the boy was indeed ill."[6] Why Kafka presented
the examination in two stages, the first superficial, the second,
more thorough, is unclear. Is it an aside to the reader: "At first
glance, there is nothing here but a fantastic story; further reading, however, will uncover unsuspected levels of significance"?
Does the timing of second stage, the discovery that the boy
is ill, to come immediately after the doctor's thoughts about
Rosa reflect the evolution of his own feelings for her, inconsequential at first, then suddenly transformed into a deep sense of
longing and grief? The relation of the two-stage medical diag-
nosis to the two phases of the doctor's emotional evolution may
be confirmed by the color of the wound he discovers: *Rosa Rot*,
rose-red.

Kafka puts great emphasis on the description of the wound:
"In his [the boy's] right side, near the hip, was an open wound
as big as the palm of my hand. Rose-red, in many variations of
the shade, dark in the hollows, lighter at the edges, softly granu-
lated, with irregular clots of blood, open as a surface mine to
the daylight. That was how it looked from a distance. But on a
closer inspection there was another complication. I could not
help a low whistle of surprise. Worms, as thick and as long as
my little finger, themselves rose-red and blood-spotted as well,
were wriggling from their fastness in the interior of the wound
toward the light, all white heads and many little legs."[7]

Some associations with the wound can probably be excluded: Jesus' side pierced, according to the legend, by the
spear of a Roman soldier or the (not unrelated) story of King

Amfortas's side wound in Richard Wagner's *Parsifal.* A more likely interpretation, as Alt shows, identifies the wound as a vagina; given the inbuilt reference to Rosa, it becomes a violent reminder of the doctor's aroused erotic pining for the faraway maid, possibly lost forever.[8] But here is the rub: the rose-red vagina that should arouse the doctor is filled with whitish worms that can only trigger disgust. Kafka's sexuality is once more barely hidden: the surge of libido is hampered by the repulsive implications of heterosexual intercourse.

What follows is again narrated in staccato style:

> And so they came, the family and the village elders, and stripped my clothes off me; a school choir with the teacher at the head of it stood before the house and sang these words to an utterly simple tune:
>
> > "Strip his clothes off, then he will heal us,
> > If he doesn't, kill him dead!
> > Only a doctor, only a doctor."
>
> Then my clothes were off and I looked at the people quietly, my fingers in my beard and my head cocked to one side. . . . They took me by the head and feet and carried me to the bed. They laid me down in it next to the wall, on the side of the wound. Then they all left the room; the door was shut; the singing stopped; clouds covered the moon; the bedding was warm around me; the horses' heads in the open windows wavered like shadows.[9]

At first, the scene evokes a shamanistic healing ritual. The link between the scene and some sacred ceremony is indirectly announced by the sentences just preceding the stripping off of the doctor's clothes. The boy has whispered to him: "Will you save me?" And the doctor's thoughts have turned again toward his demanding patients and Rosa the maid: "That is what people are like in my district. Always expecting the impossible from the doctor. They have lost their ancient beliefs, the parson sits at home and unravels his vestments, one after another; but the doctor is supposed to be omnipotent with his merciful surgeon's hand. Well, as it pleases them; I have not thrust my services on them; if they misuse me for sacred ends, I let that happen to me too; what better do I want, old country doctor that I am, bereft of my servant girl!"[10]

The evocation of "lost" ancient beliefs and of the parson who sits at home is an allusion to dwindling Christian faith, but the notion of misusing the doctor "for sacred ends" probably points to magical healing practices, which oblige the doctor to lie with the patient. A diary entry of June 2, 1916, a few months before Kafka wrote "A Country Doctor," indicates that he had just read Nathan Soederblom's *Das Werden des Gottesglaubens* (The evolution of religious faith) and was particularly interested in some beliefs about medicine men among Australian tribes.[11]

What follows is left hazy. The ritual apparently demands a symbolic "wedding night" between healer and patient; in the story, the appearances point to its make-believe aspect but imbue it nonetheless with ambiguous significance. Once the doctor lies in the boy's bed, the "couple" remains alone: "Then, they all left the room; the door was shut; the singing stopped . . ." Even nature adds to the mystical dimension of the event: "clouds covered the moon." Only the two horses remain at the windows, surveying the scene. The doctor lies on the side of the vagina-like wound that evokes homosexual intercourse but also the young maid Rosa and the repelling worms.

The doctor's escape is as rapid as all the other sequences of this surreal night journey. After calming the boy with a few unctuous promises that the wound would heal ("It is really so, take the word of honor of an official doctor"), the doctor throws his clothes through one of the windows as the horses move back, crawls from the room into his carriage, and, although his fur coat has missed the mark, sets on his way. But there is no sign this time of the miraculous speed of the earlier trip.

> Slowly, like old men, we crawled through the snowy wastes; a long time echoed behind us the new but faulty song of the children:

> > "O be joyful, all you patients,
> > The doctor's laid in bed beside you!"

The mournful summing up follows: "Never shall I reach home at this rate; my flourishing practice is done for; my successor is robbing me, but in vain, for he cannot take my place; in my house the disgusting groom is raging; Rosa is his victim; I do not want to think about it anymore. Naked, exposed to the frost of this most unhappy of ages, with an earthly vehicle, unearthly horses, old man that I am, I wander astray. My fur coat is hanging from the back of the carriage, but I cannot reach it, and none of my limber pack of patients lifts a finger: Betrayed! Betrayed! A false alarm on the night bell once answered—it cannot be made good, not ever."[12]

"This most unhappy of ages" is the country doctor's verdict upon his time. As for the population to which he caters, the society in which he lives, they are nothing but a "limber pack" ready to betray anybody at any moment, even those who try to help them. The doctor's "Betrayed! Betrayed!" echoes Kurtz's "The horror! The horror!" in Joseph Conrad's *Heart of Darkness*. Written some seventeen years apart, both texts denounce the same European civilization, shown in Conrad's novella as responsible for the abominations of colonialism and in Kafka's story—written in the midst of the First World War—as hiding atavistic brutality behind the pretense of progress: "Kill him dead! Only a doctor, only a doctor."[13]

Yet, what of the doctor himself? What of the symbol of

progress and modernity: the physician? Kafka showed a clear preference for various forms of what nowadays we would call "alternative medicine," as well as vegetarianism, special ways of chewing food (the Fletcher method), and daily exercise according to the teachings of the Danish guru Jens Peder Müller. He dabbled in nudism, took up gardening (for therapeutic purposes), and, more generally speaking, could be considered as a devotee of the "back to nature" movement that spread through Europe under the most diverse guises in the first decades of the twentieth century. In the text, the doctor is not described as advocating primitive healing practices, but, as he puts it: "If they misuse me for sacred ends, I let that happen to me too." Whatever significance one may give to this sentence, as an expression either of acquiescence or of desperation, the story unveils how the powerful remnants of a premodern world permeate the thin layer of civilization.

In this civilization of brutality, the doctor has literally lost his way. Unable to make a stand from the very outset and throughout the story, the doctor is set on his fatal ride by the groom's signal, undressed and carried into the patient's bed by the family and the village elders, and finally dragged into the wilderness by his wayward horses. The protagonist's loss of direction and his endless wandering echo motifs of two other stories written at the same time as "A Country Doctor": "The Bucket Rider" and "The Hunter Gracchus," also tales of passivity and submission to uncontrollable and chaotic forces.

It has often been suggested that "A Country Doctor" was influenced by a collection of legends of Polish Jews translated and edited by Alexander Eliasberg in 1916 that Kafka read in the same year. One of the stories tells of a wonder rabbi called from afar (the physician of the king of Prussia) to attend to a dying young patient in some shtetl. Wonder horses carry the *Maggid* in an instant. He recognizes that the patient is beyond help and wants to leave, but the assembled community blocks his way and the patient begs him to stay: "Your presence is what heals me." The Maggid answers that the physician's presence heals only because next to him stands an angel.[14]

Another source, less esoteric but no less miraculous, could be Gustave Flaubert's story *La Légende de Saint Julien L'Hospitalier*. In this short masterpiece, which Kafka had read, we discover the life of a sinner, a murderous nobleman, who, on becoming aware of the evil in him, abandons all his riches and henceforth lives as a ferryman on the bank of a large river. During a stormy night he hears a voice calling for help from the other shore. He sets on his way and ferries a dying leper to the safety of his hut. The leper begs Julien to lie next to him and hold him for warmth; as he dies the leper becomes Christ, who carries Julien in his arms to heaven.

While these two stories may have offered Kafka concrete details for his own "healer's tale," other potential sources may have crossed Kafka's mind: Flaubert's Charles Bovary, the weak and submissive husband of Emma Bovary is a country doctor. Moreover, in the story as it is told here, Rosa is the symbol of life, of emotional awakening for the old man. Kafka links the wound to Rosa by describing its color: rose-red (*"Rosa Rot"*). If the wound can be identified as a vagina, the story keeps its internal coherence; yet, the wound as such—a wound that cannot be healed—is also a symbol of death or of irretrievable misery. How, then, can it be linked to Rosa the maid?

There is a well-known Czech and Jewish legend about the most famous Jew from Prague (after Kafka), the sixteenth-century rabbi Yehuda Loew, who created the Golem, his formidable servant made of clay. Rabbi Loew, also called the Maharal, according to the Hebrew acronym of the Rabbi's name and appellation, had lived a very long life (probably till age ninety-five) when a little girl offered him a rose; the fragrance of the rose caused his demise. As uplifting as the legend may be, it nonetheless links the rose to death.[15]

The two most commonly cited sources, Flaubert's Saint Julien and Eliasberg, offered Kafka the material for a perfectly ironic reworking: in his story, there is no healing, no angel, and no Christ; the two horses are no heavenly messengers but rather creatures from hell, and the doctor, who barely escapes the village with his life, finds himself dragged into snowy wilderness, possibly forever.

In choosing his story of a country doctor, Kafka must have thought of a real country doctor, his favorite uncle Siegfried Löwy, the bachelor physician living in a small Moravian town, whom Franz often visited in his student days. Such a Jewish doctor amid a Christian peasant population may have been surrounded by any number of legends and even by intimations of hostility and violence (the "open blue-eyed face" of the groom may well have been a metonymy for the surrounding peasant society). Be this as it may, the doctor in Kafka's story has often been interpreted as the Wandering Jew of Christian lore, condemned to the misery of an eternal life of aimless roaming through a hostile world, a life that no death could redeem.

2

In *Kafka's Clothes*, Mark Anderson has drawn attention to the central significance of clothing in the author's world of symbols: whether the inspiration came from the book of Genesis or from Kafka Sr.'s store of clothing accessories (*Galanteriewaren*), for Franz Kafka clothes meant the world of appearances. Undressing, the shedding of these appearances, the move toward self-liberation from all make-believes, can mean "being in a human world and struggling to reach a sacred realm beyond it" or, from the perspective of the writer, the stripping off of "all the false coverings of the empirical self, in search for 'the undying fire' of the aesthetic truth."[16]

Before starting on his fateful journey, the old doctor stands immobile, twice covered up: in his heavy clothes and his fur coat ("muffled in furs") and "with the snow gathering more and more thickly upon me . . ." The outer blanket of snow, of a white shroud, could be an intimation of death. The doctor is alive but desperate, forlorn and emotionally dead.

Surreal forces intervene, and within moments, the doctor's carriage stands in front of the patient's farmyard. In the sickroom the air is "un-breathable," and although the doctor considers the possibility of cutting the visit short, he allows the undressing process to start: "Yet, I permitted the patient's sister, who fancied that I was dazed by the heat, to take my fur coat from me."[17] When the doctor, who believes at first that nothing is wrong with the young patient, motions for his fur coat as he prepares to leave, he does not get the coat back but rather has to face the truth: the worm-infested side wound.

Peeling off the appearances becomes then brutally rapid: "Strip the clothes off, then he will heal us / If he doesn't, kill him dead! / Only a doctor, only a doctor."[18] As rapidly as his clothes, the doctor sheds his most fundamental beliefs about the world surrounding him and about himself. He recognizes that the status that was his — district doctor — is ultimately worthless in the eyes of the populace; he discovers the failure of traditional religion and the permanence of the most primitive sacrificial cults; he cannot, in hearing the choir, but admit the murderous evil that permeates the world, and, on the most personal level, he is starkly confronted with his own ambiguous sexual drives: Rosa the maid on the one hand but the young man with whom he now lies in bed, "on the side of the wound," on the other hand.

The most puzzling aspect of the story occurs during the doctor's escape; a set of minor details adds an entirely new dimension to the symbolic significance of the tale. "Now it was time for me to think of escaping. The horses were still standing faithfully in their places. My clothes, my fur coat, my bag were quickly collected; I didn't want to waste time dressing; if the horses raced home as they had come, I should only be springing, as it were, out of this bed into my own. Obediently a horse backed away from the window; I threw the bundle into the carriage; the fur coat missed its mark and was caught on a hook only by the sleeve. Good enough. I swung myself onto the horse. With the reins loosely trailing, one horse barely fastened to the other, the carriage swaying behind, my fur coat last of all in the snow . . ."[19] The same theme is insistently repeated a few lines later, in the closing segment of the story: "My fur coat is hanging from the back of the carriage, but I cannot reach it, and none of the limber pack of patients lifts a finger . . ."[20]

Within the more general category of clothing and nakedness symbols, the fur coat is becoming the central element as the story moves to its end. During the first part of the story, the fur coat conveys the protective function of appearances, of the accepted lies of worldly existence. It protects the old doctor from the snow that accumulates around him and keeps open the possibility that he will notice the beautiful maid Rosa, the carrier of a new life.

Alas, during his hasty escape the doctor retrieves the coat but does not manage to throw it into the carriage. He has missed the mark, a sad summary of his entire life. If he hoped to return to the cozy life of appearances, his inability to reach the coat, compounded by the sluggish stride of the horses (like old men—after coitus) and the wayward traveling through the snowy wasteland, shatters all such hope.

Uncovering the truth about oneself and about the evil at the core of humankind could have become the first step to redemption; in Kafka's world, though, truth seems to open the gates of annihilation.

3

The evolution of the country doctor's fate is replicated at several levels of the story; at each level the premise and the outcome are similar, but at each level a new element is added to the symbolic meaning of the narrative, a new perspective is unveiled. Thus, at the level considered in this segment, the patient's words are an echo of the doctor's story but with an independent moment of revelation at the very end.

Let us recall the initial encounter between doctor and patient, as told by the doctor: "The youngster heaved himself up from under the feather bedding, threw his arms around my neck, and whispered in my ear: 'Doctor, let me die.' I glanced around the room; no one had heard it. . . . The boy kept clutching at me from his bed to remind me of his entreaty . . ." As the doctor notices upon entering the room, the boy has not suffered from some sudden attack; in fact, he does not look ill at all: "Gaunt, without any fever, not cold, not warm, with vacant eyes . . ." Thus the entreaty of the youngster for death must come from some deep despair, from some utter forlornness not unlike that of the doctor himself at the beginning of the story. Soon after this exchange the doctor's thoughts reveal what his state of mind has been long before this fateful night: "I wanted to die too. . . . I had once more been called needlessly, I was used to that, the whole district made my life a torment with my night bell . . ."[21]

Suddenly, the boy's mood changes: the doctor, on a second examination, discovers the large wound in his side, teeming with worms. The physician immediately understands that there is no hope: "Poor boy, you were past helping. I had discovered your great wound; this blossom in your side was destroying you . . ." Of course, the youngster knows nothing of the doctor's thoughts. "'Will you save me?' whispered the boy with a sob, quite blinded by the life within his wound." The boy's unexpected surge of hope, due probably to the discovery of his wound by the doctor, coincides with the old man's sudden urge to see his maid again. In both cases there is longing for a new life, there is an abrupt and simultaneous emotional awakening. It won't last long.[22]

The doctor is undressed and laid upon the boy's bed. The youngster's mood has changed again, from hope to disillusion, anger, even hatred, as the doctor relates: "'Do you know,' said a voice in my ear, 'I have very little confidence in you. Why, you were only blown in here, you didn't come on your own feet. What I would like best is to scratch your eyes out.'" The doctor attempts to apologize, which brings the following retort: "Am I supposed to be content with this apology? Oh, I must be, I can't help it. I always have to put up with things. A fine wound is all I brought into the world; that was my sole endowment."

"A fine wound is all I brought into the world." It is original sin that the boy is describing; he carries the visible sign of what in his environment is probably considered the common human condition. The doctor has also been guilty of a sin, only at this point revealed to him: emotional inertia. At his own level, the doctor is as sick as his patient and, by then, for him no healing will be possible anymore.

The last exchange between the doctor and the boy opens with a strange metaphor and moves to an outright lie. After the boy's desperate statement that the wound is his sole endowment, the doctor's answer is anything but truthful: "'My young friend,' said I, 'your mistake is: you have not a wide enough view. I have been in all the sickrooms, far and wide, and I tell you: your wound is not so bad. Done in a corner with two strikes from an axe. Many a one proffers his side and can hardly hear the axe in the forest, far less that it is coming nearer to him.' 'Is that really so, or are you deluding me in my fever?' 'It is really so, take the word of honor of an official doctor.' And he took it and lay still."[23]

The doctor's lie can be dismissed as an attempt to protect the teenager from understanding the hopelessness of his state. Yet the story implies that the doctor lies for purely egoistic reasons: to keep the boy quiet so that he may leave: "And he took it and lay still. But now it was time for me to think of escaping . . ." The doctor's lie echoes the villagers' readiness to kill him.

The story leaves no doubt about the doctor's feelings for his district's patients in general and this family in particular: he resents and despises them. When he arrives at the patient's farm, the father offers him a glass of his precious rum: "A glass of rum was poured out for me, the old man clapped me on the shoulder, a familiarity justified by this offer of his treasure. I shook my head; in the narrow confines of the old man's thoughts I felt ill; that was my only reason for refusing the drink."[24] The "narrow confines" will find their equivalent in the subsequent words the doctor addresses to the son: "Your mistake is: you have not a wide enough view."

Rum had been offered to warm the body and the heart in this deep winter weather; it is shunned, as Rosa has been shunned and as the patient will be shunned. The doctor's feelings for his fellow humans remain suppressed, and the doctor flees the patient's house as dead-alive as he has been from the outset, and thus as dead-alive he will wander astray in the endless wintry night of a deserted world.

In "A Country Doctor," the doctor, though with whip in hand, nonetheless abandons his young maid Rosa to the violent sexual onslaught of the groom. In *The Trial*, Joseph K. opens the door of a lumber room in his bank and discovers a whipper lashing the two warders who initially had come to arrest him. K. abandons the warders to their fate, and hastily so, when, a second time, he opens the same door and discovers the same scene.[25]

In both episodes, the main character abandons others to blatant violence. In "A Country Doctor," the responsibility is heavier than in *The Trial*, but in both cases the ever hidden supreme authority (or what the characters imagine as such) inflicts a punishment (that may also be read as self-punishment, unconsciously called for to atone for a grave moral lapse). Did Kafka create "A Country Doctor" to stress the issue that appeared first in *The Trial*? Did he feel a secret "satisfaction" in pondering about the dark fate of the country doctor with whom he may well have identified?

4

In the desolate world of Kafka's fiction, atmospheric stage props convey the "mood" of the narrative (darkness, night, snow, fog, and rain): the main scenes in "Description of a Struggle" and "Wedding Preparations in the Country" take place in the rain and darkness of night; Joseph K.'s walk to the execution place in *The Trial* and K.'s arrival in *The Castle* both are set in nighttime; and, of course, snow and night dominate the stage design of "A Country Doctor." In one case—"In the Penal Colony"—the sun glares on a torture machine and its victim(s) in the unbearable tropical heat of a barren island.

Indoor spaces are often cramped like the squalid attics where, in *The Trial*, the court, its offices, and its officials, lawyers, and defendants spend most of their time; for newcomers, breathing soon becomes difficult. For the country doctor, "In the sick room the air was almost un-breathable; the neglected stove was smoking; I wanted to push open the window but first I had to look at my patient."[26] This repeated use of suggestive images may have resulted from an ongoing influence of Expressionism or even from contemporary fantastic literature, such as Gustav Meyrink's *Der Golem*, which Kafka knew well but disliked.[27]

But Kafka wouldn't be Kafka if all signs were easily accessible. Thus, in "A Country Doctor," the snow accumulating around the old doctor reminds the reader of a shroud that may well be a portent of things to come; in *The Metamorphosis*, the father bombards Gregor with apples, one of which remains fatally stuck in the son's back. Apples? There is sin in the Samsa family, some deeply hidden "original sin." And, in *The Trial*, before the most enigmatic scene of the novel—the meeting in the cathedral between the prison chaplain, speaking in riddles, and Joseph K.—the protagonist is introduced, in the office of the bank director, to an Italian client and tourist; he is supposed to serve as guide to the cathedral for this figure, who speaks a local dialect of Italian that Joseph K. is utterly unable to understand.

One could regress further to an array of signs more thoroughly camouflaged, to evanescent traces of the past that become portents of the future barely visible, never entirely decipherable, at times intentionally misleading. As Kafka expressed it in one of his aphorisms: "The true way is along a rope that is not spanned high in the air, but only just above the ground. It seems intended more to cause stumbling than to be walked along."[28] Kafka, no doubt, was alluding to a rope he had himself spanned to show us the way.

When we consider plot, we recognize the repetitive use of a central element: the existence of an unidentified source of threat and ill omen. In the "Country Doctor," the sudden and surreal appearance in the pigsty of the groom and the horses means that they were sent by such an unknown entity that suddenly, by intention or chance, focused on the doctor or had been watching him as a choice victim. In *The Trial* the accused, Joseph K., and the people around him never get the slightest glimpse of the higher authority that rules over the courts, issues the arrest warrant, and dictates the outcome of the "judicial" process: "Where was the Judge," K. shouts before his execution, "whom he had never seen? Where was the high Court to which he had never penetrated?"[29] And, what was the Law? In *The Castle*, the supreme authority, recognized by all but never seen and never described, Count Westwest, is as abstract and as blindly potent as the law or the supreme judge in *The Trial*. Are we facing an absent God, a hidden evil demiurge, or blind fate?

Whereas in everyday life an unexpected event that interferes with daily routine can be inconsequential (or have diverse consequences), in Kafka's fiction unexpected and puzzling openings regularly announce the onset of a dire series of consequences. "I was in great perplexity": thus starts the story told by the country doctor. Just as he has been called to the village ten miles away, his horse has died. The death of the horse, the initial disconcerting event, announces, incidentally, the passing of normal, earthly life; soon thereafter, the appearance of the two unearthly horses signals the shift of the events unto an entirely different realm. Such initial perplexity, caused by a break in the habitual routine, marks the beginning of *The Trial*. When Joseph K. wakes up, on the morning of his thirtieth birthday, he notices to his astonishment that his landlady's cook, who every morning at eight brought him his breakfast, had not come. "This had never happened," he comments. When he rings, instead of the cook a man enters the room and informs Joseph K. that he is under arrest.[30]

In *The Metamorphosis*, as Gregor Samsa awakens, ready to start the day, he discovers that getting out of bed could be a problem: overnight, he has become a huge bug; as he lays on his back, "his numerous legs wave helplessly before his eyes."[31]

A complex hierarchy of higher and lower officials seems to be set in motion by the force at the center of the mysterious spiderweb, down to the emissaries who watch the victim at each turn of the twisted path leading to his downfall. Usually the surveillance is undertaken by two apparently lower beings. Thus, in "A Country Doctor," the two surreal horses carry the doctor to the patient's farm, then push the window open when he is in the sickroom to observe the full sequence of events. With him, thereafter, they wander into the snowy desert.

The two horses have been preceded by the two warders and the two executioners in *The Trial*, and they will be succeeded by the two notorious assistants in *The Castle*. Once the higher powers have chosen their victim, they will follow his every step on the road to perdition. Even the two celluloid balls that pursue the old bachelor in the eponymous story are behind his every move, and when they are tricked out of their surveillance, his two office aides take over.

The ominous surveillance usually takes place in the midst of a larger crowd either staring at or surrounding the main character, never in a friendly way. The ever-present "other's gaze," a later tenet of French existentialism, is a repeated fixture in Kafka's texts. Neighbors gather around the family, in the sickroom, while the doctor is examining the wound and the village elders join to strip the doctor's clothes, while "a school choir with the teacher at the head of it stood before the house."[32]

At the very beginning of *The Trial*, as Joseph K. wakes up and before he has heard about his arrest, he notices "from his pillow the old lady opposite, who seemed to be peering at him with a curiosity unusual even for her . . ."[33] Soon thereafter, as K. moves to the adjacent room and is caught up in confrontation with the two warders, "through the open window he had another glimpse of the old woman, who with truly senile inquisitiveness had moved along to the window exactly opposite, in order to go on seeing all that could be seen."[34] Soon there are three observers at the window on the other side of the street, and the two warders have been joined by an inspector. Worse, as K. discovered to his amazement, three clerks from his bank have been present throughout his interrogation by the inspector, without his noticing them. And so it goes, to the very end of the novel, when the two men who execute the death sentence watch his last moment: "But the hands of one of the partners were already at K.'s throat, while the other thrust the knife deep into his heart and turned it there twice. With failing eyes K. could still see the two of them immediately before him, cheek leaning against cheek, watching the final act."[35]

In *The Castle*, everybody observes K., even the lowly peasants patronizing the modest inn where he has found a place to sleep. "Yet before long he was awakened. A young man in city clothes, with an actor's face, narrow eyes, thick eyebrows, stood beside him with the landlord. The peasants, too, were still there, a few had turned their chairs around to see and hear better."[36]

No intimacy is possible between K. and his instant lover, Frieda. They make love after K. dismisses the assistants for the day, but when they are about to get up, the assistants are crouching in the corner of the room, apparently having remained there throughout; "in addition to that, the landlady was sitting by the bed, knitting a sock, a small task ill-suited for her huge frame, which almost darkened the room."[37] Somehow, "the others" are always there in Kafka's texts. "L'enfer, c'est les autres"—Hell is other people—Sartre has one of his characters declare in *Huis-Clos*. Kafka had preceded him by twenty years.

In its general significance, the others' gaze aims at reducing an individual to an object. In Kafka's stories, this ever-present intrusion carries an additional meaning: there is a secret to be uncovered, something that the protagonist attempts to hide. Doesn't this recurrent metaphor bring us back to Kafka's constant efforts to hide his sexual leanings? As just mentioned, the two assistants (and the landlady) watch K. and Frieda making love, and the two horses in "A Country Doctor" continue eyeing the Doctor as he lies in bed with his young patient, "on the side of the wound."

In "A Country Doctor," the constant reversal of expected norms creates the feeling of disorientation: the groom who should obey immediately turns into the figure of power and authority, while the doctor who represents authority (and has the whip in hand) becomes meek and subservient; the doctor who responds to summons in a midwinter night feels only contempt for and hostility toward his patients; the young man who expects help from the doctor declares eventually that he wishes to scratch his eyes out; the patient's family and community who awaited a miracle from science turn to ancestral rituals, brutalize the doctor, and threaten to kill him.

In the story that epitomizes the thrust of Kafka's work (and that he particularly liked) there is no escape. The innocent victims are destroyed: Rosa will be raped and subjugated by the groom, while the young patient will waste away, doomed by the wound inflicted upon him at birth. As for the doctor, whatever our verdict may be, his fate is worse than death: no dying can relieve the Wandering Jew. Only unrestrained violence (by the groom, the villagers, and the world) survives and possibly thrives.

Within the context of this story, there is no "grace," and no redemption. While Flaubert's "La Légende de St Julien" is a naïve story of salvation represented on the painted windows of a village church, and while Eliasberg's wonder rabbi carried by miraculous horses is but a demonstration of the greatness of God and the powers of his faithful servants, in Kafka's "night journey" nothing remains but darkness: surreal forces and earthly drives seem to work in unison.

5

The Writer and His Worlds

"You have no idea, Felice," Kafka wrote to her on July 8, 1913, "what havoc literature creates in certain heads. It is like monkeys leaping about in the treetops, instead of staying firmly on the ground. It is being lost and not being able to help it. What can one do?"[1]

Can literature save him or destroy him? Or save him by destroying him? Kafka doesn't know. "All I possess," he told Felice in June of the same year, "are certain powers which, at a depth almost inaccessible under normal conditions, shape themselves into literature, powers to which, however, in my present professional as well as physical state, I dare not commit myself, because for every inner exhortation of these powers there are as many, if not more inner warnings. Could I but commit myself to them they would undoubtedly, of this I am convinced, lift me out of my inner misery in an instant."[2]

Kafka clearly perceived the incompatibility between writing and a "normal" life (even if his arguments were meant in part to dissuade Felice from any long-term commitment). Thus a few days after speaking of "certain powers . . . which shape themselves into literature," he returned to the necessary conditions for writing: "My attitude to my writing and my attitude to people is interchangeable; it is a part of my nature, and not due to temporary circumstances. What I need for my writing is seclusion, not "like a hermit," that would not be enough, but like the dead. Writing, in this sense, is a sleep deeper than that of death, and just as one would not and cannot tear the dead from their graves, so I must not and cannot be torn from my desk at night. This has no immediate bearing on my relation with people; it is simply that I can write only in this regular, continuous, and rigorous fashion, and therefore can live only in this way too."[3]

I

Seclusion and silence could never last for long. "I sit in my room in the headquarters of all the noise in the whole flat," Kafka wrote in November 1911.

> I hear all the doors banging, all this noise only spares me the footsteps of those walking between them, I even hear the slamming of the oven door in the kitchen. Father bursts through the doors of my room and walks across it, his dressing-gown trailing behind him. Somebody is scraping the ash from the stove next door. Valli asks, shouting each word across the front room, whether father's hat has been cleaned already and a hiss, which is well intentioned towards me, heightens the screaming answer. The front door handle is pushed down with a noise like that coming from a catarrh-infected throat, then the door opens wide, sounding like a female voice, and finally shuts again with a dull, male thump, which sounds the most inconsiderate of all. Father is gone

and the gentler, more absent-minded and hopeless noise starts, introduced by the voices of the two canaries. I had thought it before; now the two canaries make me think again, whether it would not be a good idea to open the door a tiny bit, slither into the neighbouring room like a snake and from the floor beg my sisters and their nanny to be quiet.[4]

Kafka's sensitivity to noise plagued him throughout his life. It explains the strange schedule (writing during the quiet hours of the night) that he described to Felice soon after the beginning of their correspondence: "From 8 to 2 or 2:30 in the office, then lunch till 3 or 3:30, after that sleep in bed (usually only attempts . . .) till 7:30, then ten minutes of exercises, naked at the open window, then an hour's walk—alone, with Max or with another friend, then dinner with my family . . . ; then at 10:30 (but not often till 11:30) I sit down to write, and I go on, depending on my strength, inclination and luck, until 1, 2 or 3 o'clock, once even till 6 in the morning. Then again exercises, as above, but of course avoiding all exertions, a wash, and then, usually with a slight pain in my heart and twitching stomach muscles, to bed. Then every imaginable effort to get to sleep."[5]

During the same year, 1912, before even considering any plans of marriage, a prescient Kafka used his "writing schedule" to hint at his inability to live a normal conjugal life. In November 1912, he quoted to Felice an eighteenth-century Chinese poem written by Yüan-Tzu-Tsai:

> In the Dead of Night
> In the cold night, while poring over my book,
> I forgot the hour of bedtime.
> The scent of my gold-embroidered bedcover
> Has already evaporated,
> The fire in the hearth burns no more.
> My beautiful mistress, who hitherto has controlled
> Her wrath with difficulty, snatches away the lamp,
> And asks: Do you know how late it is?[6]

On February 9, 1915, Kafka rented a room on the Bilekgasse; the next day, though, the torture was back: "First evening. My neighbour talks for hours with the landlady. Both speak softly, the landlady almost inaudibly, and therefore so much the worse. My writing, which has been coming along for the last two days, is interrupted, who knows for how long a time? Absolute despair. Is it like this in every house? Does such ridiculous and absolutely killing misery await me with every landlady in every city?"[7]

Kafka moved again, but to no avail. "Harassed by noise," he complained in March.

> A beautiful, much more friendly room than the one on Bilekgasse. . . . But a great deal of noise from the carriages down below; however, I am growing quite used to it. But impossible for me to grow used to the noise in the afternoon. From time to time a crash in the kitchen or in the corridor. Yesterday, in the attic above, perpetual rolling of a ball, as if someone for some incomprehensible reason were bowling, then a piano below me in addition. Yesterday evening a relative silence, worked somewhat hopefully ("Assistant Attorney"), today began with joy, suddenly, next door or below me, a party taking place, loud and fluctuating as though I were in its midst. Contended with the noise awhile, then lay on the sofa with nerves virtually shattered, silence after ten o'clock, but can't work any longer.[8]

And so it went . . .

Noise wasn't the only torture. Kafka was a hypochondriac who magnified a variety of minor ailments such as headaches, upset stomach, and, of course, insomnia—until, in August 1917, tuberculosis set in. Yet whatever the intensity of the early ailments may have been, his fixation upon their constant presence left him incapable of writing for days and weeks on end; this was the internal noise that competed with the external "din" and, for years, turned his daily life into a constant struggle to salvage a minimum of quiet. And there was another obstacle, a major one: the office.

In the letter of June 1913 to Felice in which he declared that to write he needed to be "like the dead," Kafka addressed the issue of his job. "The office? That one day I shall be in a position to leave is quite out of the question. But that I shall one day be forced to leave it, on account of being unfit to carry on, that is by no means out of the question. In this respect my feeling of inner insecurity and anxiety is terrible, and here again the only and actual reason for it is my writing. . . . Writing and office cannot be reconciled, since writing has its center of gravity in depth, whereas the office is on the surface of life. So it goes up and down, and one is bound to be torn asunder in the process." [9]

Kafka repeatedly bemoaned his daily office chores, although he was highly regarded and was regularly promoted until, on the eve of his forced retirement, he had become one of the senior employees in the (by then Czech) Workmen's Insurance Institute. Not only did he process legal cases against companies that did not fulfill their obligations under the expanding workers' insurance legislation of the empire but he participated in the drafting of substantial documentation in this domain, also dealing with rules for the use of dangerous machinery. During the war he was exempted from military service on grounds of indispensability in "matters of public interest." Soon he became involved in the handling of matters involving disabled veterans that, in 1915, had officially become the responsibility of his Insurance Institute. In that context Kafka participated in the consultations regarding the establishment of a psychiatric hospital for shell-shocked war veterans. [10]

Kafka's office work familiarized him with modern bureaucracy, its ever expanding tentacles, its increasingly unintelligible language, its altogether apparent and hidden power structures, and the like. But it seems that he himself did not recognize the incidental literary advantages of this milieu as he repeatedly asked for sick leave and even discussed with his director the possibility of quitting. Ultimately, he stayed until the summer of 1922.

In late 1911, Franz's brother-in-law Karl Hermann, Elli's husband, bought an asbestos factory in Prague. Franz later argued that he acquired a share in it—thus becoming a silent partner—because of his father's pressure; it seems in fact that it was Franz himself who pushed for the venture and involved his father in it.[11] A year later, just as Franz was working on *Amerika* and could expect two peaceful weeks during his annual leave, Karl went on a business trip and Franz, the silent partner, was expected to manage the enterprise. This time it was Franz's mother who insisted. Whether, as Franz wrote to Brod on October 7, 1912, he actually contemplated suicide ("I stood for a long time at the window and pressed against the pane and there were many moments when it should have suited me to alarm the toll collector on the bridge by my fall . . ."), his friend was worried enough to intercede with Kafka's mother.[12]

After the incident, Kafka continued writing the second version of *Amerika;* it progressed as his work typically did. "Yesterday, I had to force myself to finish the sixth chapter, and so it turned out crude and bad. I had to exclude two characters who should have entered into the chapter. So all the while I was writing, they were pursuing me, and since in the novel they were supposed to raise their arms and clench their fists, they threatened me with the same gestures."[13]

To write, Kafka needed "seclusion . . . like the dead." But to survive he needed the world: the emotional support of friends (male and female), the give and take of ideas, at least within his small group of intimates—in short, the demands and challenges of life as such.

During his years at the university, Kafka had regularly attended the meetings of the Section for Literature and Art of the "Halle"—Lese- und Redehalle der Deutschen Studenten in Prag, the Reading and Lecture Hall of German Students in Prague—a liberal German students' organization with a sizable Jewish membership. The nationalist German students had seceded from the Halle and established their own organization, Germania, in 1892. At the turn of the century a small group of Jewish students established the Zionist student organization Bar Kochba, a challenge to the Halle for the allegiance of Jewish students.[14] Kafka remained at the Halle, and in October 1902, at a meeting of the Section for Literature and Art, he became acquainted with Brod. Brod had given a lecture on Schopenhauer and Nietzsche, strongly critical of Nietzsche. Kafka vehemently disagreed and said as much to the Schopenhauer fan while he was walking home with him.

Before that evening, Brod reminisced, he had barely noticed Kafka: "He used to take part in every meeting of the 'section,' but until then we had hardly taken notice of each other. It would indeed have been difficult to notice him, because he so seldom opened his mouth, and because his outward appearance was above all deeply unobtrusive—even his elegant suits, which were mostly dark blue, were as unobtrusive and reserved as himself."[15] Soon a group of like-minded friends started meeting; later Brod wrote of them as the "Prague circle." The historian Scott Spector has shown that there was not *one* Prague Circle but rather a whole array of intersecting groups whose members knew each other and influenced one another.[16] For Kafka, however, to the extent that he participated in any such group, "the Prague Circle" was mainly the one he shared with Brod, Felix Weltsch, Oskar Baum, and a few others.

The members of the Circle—Kafka sporadically among

them—were all eager participants in the wider Prague intellectual and artistic life that, at the beginning of the century, was open to debates about a whole array of contemporary issues. Freud's theories were discussed in Max and Bertha Fanta's salon, a remarkable meeting place for the intellectual who's who of the city. At Café Louvre, a group of devotees met regularly to study Franz von Brentano's psychology of intentionality, which dominated academic psychology both in Vienna and Prague during these years. In Prague, Brentano's influence was compounded by the teachings of several of his disciples at Charles University: the philosopher Anton Marty and the psychologist Christian von Ehrenfels, one of the founders of gestalt psychology.

Kafka audited Ehrenfels's courses during two semesters at the time of his studies, and in 1913, he attended an Ehrenfels seminar. Still later, he apparently was quite impressed by what Brod wrote to him about the Prague teacher: "Your mention of Ehrenfels made a great impression upon me," Kafka answered from Zürau, in early April 1918. "Could you lend me the book [*Cosmogony*, published in Jena in 1916]?"[17] Both Weltsch and Brod were directly influenced by Ehrenfels's theories about free will, but Kafka remained an interested outsider, as he was with most theoretical systems.

Beliefs about the occult were also widespread and both Theosophy and Gnosticism apparently were among the topics debated at the Fantas'. Regarding Theosophy, particularly Rudolf Steiner's brand of Theosophy (soon to become Anthroposophy), we have Kafka's own testimony. Some scholars, however, have argued that Kafka was drawn to Gnosticism: "My Kafka is an ecstatic," Stanley Corngold states in the preface to his *Lambent Traces*. ". . . All of Kafka's writing turns on this ecstasy—its hiddenness, its warning, its power to justify a ruined life—but it cannot name directly what is nothing in respect to material things and the signs dependent on them." Influenced by the emphatic thesis of the Kafka scholar Walter Sokel, among others, Corngold mentions "types of Gnostic teaching rampant in Prague in Kafka's lifetime."[18]

There is, however, no direct mention of Gnostic ideas either in Kafka's *Diaries* or in his *Letters*, nor is there any reference to Walter Köhler's volume on Gnosticism that was found in his library. The only hypothetical basis for the assumption that Kafka was familiar with such esoteric teachings is linked to the Fantas' salon. Whereas we know that Kafka attended several of the lectures given there by the founder of Anthroposophy, Rudolf Steiner, and in March 1911 even had a private audience with him, there is no trace of Kafka's presence at any lectures or discussions on Gnosticism.[19]

In other words, the sole assumption for attributing an influence to Gnostic teachings upon Kafka's writings resides in finding in them a latent worldview showing similarities to Gnostic texts; it may or may not be a sign of direct influence, but that worldview—particularly the belief in an evil demiurge—has, of course, a coherence of its own in Kafka's work. It could be called Kafka's private Gnosticism.

Absence of evidence of a direct link does not demonstrate that Kafka was immune to ideas so widespread in his intellectual environment. There, however, lies the difficulty. The kind of Gnosticism apparently prevalent in Prague during those years was Marcionism, the doctrine of a second-century Christian heretic, Marcion. Like all Gnostics, Marcion believed in two deities, a higher God, the one proclaimed by Jesus and Paul—the God of Christianity—and an inferior creator God, the one of Jewish scriptures, Jehovah.[20] If Kafka was influenced by Prague Gnosticism, then, in his eyes, the Jewish God must have been the vengeful and evil God of the law, not the God of love. Max Brod was aware of the difficulty and argued that although his friend followed such a negative path for a long time, he ultimately turned toward a message of salvation.[21] Stanley

Corngold tries to get around the issue by finding a decisive difference between Prague Gnosticism and Marcionism—a distinction not recognized by the historian William Johnston,
who, on the contrary, affirms that Prague was under the sway
of Marcion's ideas.[22] At least one important Kafka commen-
tator, Günther Anders, fully accepts Kafka's Marcionism and
its corollaries.[23] In any case, the notion of an evil demiurge fits
Kafka's view of the human predicament.

Kafka's relationship with Max Brod was in many ways exceptional. From 1908 or so, the two friends confided to each
other matters of the heart and of the mind. At the same time,
Brod energetically promoted his shy and reticent friend. He
wrote glowing reviews about Kafka's very sporadic publications and convinced publishers of his friend's greatness. Their
friendship knew ups and downs, but it endured throughout
Kafka's life. Then Brod became the (at times problematic)
guardian of Kafka's posthumous fame.

Brod had published his own first volume of stories in 1906,
Death to the Dead, and never stopped publishing book after book,
article after article, to the end of his life. What Kafka thought
of Brod's stream of writings isn't clear. He showed interest in
each new publication or each new manuscript Brod sent him,
but it is difficult to believe that he would not have recognized
the mediocre quality of his friend's output, notwithstanding
its public success. Brod's suggestion that they should write a
novel in common ("Richard and Samuel") was dropped after
an initial attempt. Moreover, it appears certain that notwithstanding some vague similarities, Brod's literary productions
had no influence on Kafka's fiction, contrary to the unfounded
assertions of a few commentators. In any case, Brod was well
aware, from the outset, that his friend was a literary genius and
upon hearing Kafka read parts of "Wedding Preparations in the
Country," before Kafka had published a single line, he men-

tioned his name in the Berlin weekly *Die Gegenwart,* in a 1907 review essay, along with Heinrich Mann, Frank Wedekind, and Gustav Meyrink.[24]

We may consider "Shamefaced Lanky and Impure at Heart" as Kafka's first extant story. In 1903, he apparently worked on a novel that is lost. A year later, he began work on "The Description of a Struggle," followed in 1905 by "Wedding Preparations in the Country." It took until June 1909 to have "Two Conversations" (excerpted from "Description of a Struggle") published in Franz Blei's magazine *Hyperion,* and until March 1910 for the publication of five short stories (which later would be included in his first published volume, *Meditation*) in *Bohemia.*[25] But as we have seen, before anything appeared in print, Brod had already mentioned Kafka's name among those of famous contemporary writers. Thus Kafka's questions and entreaties addressed to Brod in August 1912 may appear slightly disingenuous, as he must have known the answer he would get.

"My dearest Max," Kafka wrote on August 7, 1912,

> after tormenting myself for a long time, I am stopping. I am unable and in the near future will scarcely be able to complete the remaining pieces [the texts that were to be published in *Meditation*]. Since I can't do it now, but undoubtedly will be able to do it someday, in a good spell, would you really advise me — and how could it possibly be justified? — to have something bad published with my eyes open, something which would then disgust me, like the "Conversations" in *Hyperion?* What has so far been written on the typewriter is probably not sufficient for a book, of course; but after all, is going unpublished — and [there] are probably worse outcomes — not far less bad than this damnable forcing oneself? . . . Tell me I am right! This artificial working and pondering has bothered me all along and makes me needlessly miserable. We can allow bad things to remain finally bad only on

our deathbed. Do tell me that I am right, or at least that you aren't angry with me about it. Then I shall be able to begin something else with a clear conscience and also be reassured about you.[26]

Meditation came out at the end of 1912, a year after Kafka had started work on *Amerika*. But in his eyes, the radical break-through took place in the night from September 22 to 23, 1912, when in a few hours he wrote "The Judgment." Kafka was elated and noted famously in his diary on September 23: "This story, 'The Judgment,' I wrote at one sitting, from ten o'clock at night to six o'clock in the morning. I was hardly able to pull my legs out from under the desk, they had got so stiff from sitting. The fearful strain and joy, how the story developed before me, as if I were advancing over water. Several times during this night I heaved my own weight on my back. How everything can be said, how for everything, for the strangest fancies, there waits a great fire in which they perish and rise up again. . . . Only *in this way* can writing be done, only with such coherence, with such complete opening out of the body and the soul."[27]

To Brod, Kafka declared some time later: "Do you know what the last sentence means? When I wrote it, I had in mind a violent ejaculation." In his biography, Brod quotes that last sentence, which follows the son's suicide: "At this moment passed over the bridge a truly unending stream of traffic."[28] ("Traffic" in German can also mean "intercourse.")

Later again, as Kafka was correcting the story's proofs, he confided to his diary (February 11, 1913): "The story came out of me like a real birth, covered with filth and slime, and only I have the hand that can reach to the body itself and the strength of desire to do so."[29] Incidentally, in his diary entries referring to "The Judgment," Kafka mentions having "of course" thought of Freud when writing "The Judgment"; we assume, as already mentioned, that he meant the Oedipal conflict between father and son and its most extreme result: the son's condemnation to death by his father and his ensuing suicide. We also assume that if indeed "Georg" represents Franz, as Kafka indicated in his diary, the story alludes clearly enough to that very Oedipal struggle unfolding in his relations with his own father.

But couldn't it be that Freud was even more centrally present in Kafka's story than the author himself realized, that some crucial aspects of the story stemmed from his own unconscious and were hidden from him? Kafka repeatedly acknowledged that "Georg" should be seen as the equivalent of "Franz"; nowhere did he mention, however, that it also was the name of the first of two younger brothers who died in infancy. (Georg died in December 1886.) As Kafka's biographer Peter-André Alt surmises, the mother's intense sorrow must have awakened in the surviving child feelings of "fear, guilt and envy."[30] Such "sinful" feelings may have provided additional justification for the punishment ordered by the father and readily accepted by the real-life Georg's guilt-ridden older brother—and the character Georg's alter ego—Franz.

Two years of extreme productivity (in two phases of a few months each) followed the completion of "The Judgment," as Kafka himself noted on December 31, 1914, in an unusual summing up: "Have been working since August, in general not little and not badly, yet neither in the first nor in the second respect to the limit of my ability. . . . Worked on, but did not finish: 'The Trial,' 'Memoirs of the Kalda Railway,' 'The Village Schoolmaster,' 'The Assistant Attorney,' and the beginnings of various little things. Finished only: 'In the Penal Colony' and a chapter of 'Der Verschollene' [*The Man Who Disappeared*, better known in English as *Amerika*], both during the two-week holiday. I don't know why I am drawing up this summary, it's not like me!"[31] In 1912, Kafka had already completed *The Metamorphosis*.

The years 1915 and 1916 mark a pause in Kafka's writing, although during that time he wrote "The Village Schoolmaster"

and "Blumfeld, the Old Bachelor." Then, in late 1916 and early
1917, he completed "A Country Doctor," one of a series of
stories, all written within a few months in Kafka's "hideout" on
the Alchemistengasse, a tiny lodging which his sister Ottla had
put at his disposal in one of the quaint houses on the castle hill.
Most of these stories would be published three years later in a
volume entitled *A Country Doctor.* In the meantime, two of the
texts, "Jackals and Arabs" and "A Report to the Academy," were
published in Martin Buber's periodical *Der Jude.*

During the nights of August 12 and 13, 1917, Kafka suffered
the two pulmonary hemorrhages that changed the course of his
life. First diagnosed as a bronchial inflammation, the symptoms
soon pointed to incipient tuberculosis, and Kafka was told by
his physician, Professor Friedel Pick, to settle in the country
for a while, in an attempt to restore his health. In September
1917 he moved to Zürau to Ottla's house, where he stayed until
May 1918. It is there that he started to write the aphorisms that
seem to indicate a turn to spiritual issues.[32]

Throughout these years and afterward, Kafka never ques-
tioned his vocation as a writer, but real and imagined obstacles
assailed him from all sides: "What will be my fate as a writer,"
he predicted on August 6, 1914,

> is very simple. Any talent for portraying my dreamlike inner
> life has thrust all other matters into the background; my
> life has dwindled dreadfully, and will not cease to dwindle.
> Nothing else will ever satisfy me. But the strength I can
> muster for that portrayal is not to be counted upon: perhaps
> it has already vanished forever, perhaps it will come back to
> me again, although the circumstances of my life don't favour
> its return. Thus I waver, continually fly to the summit of the
> mountain, but then fall back in a moment. Others waver too,
> but in lower regions, with greater strength; if they are in
> danger of falling, they are caught up by the kinsman who
> walks beside them for that very purpose. But I waver on

the heights; it is not death, alas, but the eternal torments of dying.[33]

Kafka's torments were unavoidable: They were, for him, an intrinsic part of creation. He said as much in the lines just quoted, and he was to be even more explicit over the years. But he also needed some kinsmen to walk beside him. Brod remained a devoted and reliable kinsman; he was a daily companion, a sounding board, and a tireless "publicist." Some of the other friends were less impressed at the outset: Werfel famously prophesied, after a first reading of early Kafka texts by Brod, that this would never get beyond Bodenbach (a border town between Bohemia and Germany).[34] These friends changed their minds.

Incidentally, Kafka's publishers were no "kinsmen" throughout, with the exception of Ernst Rowohlt, the first of them. Kurt Wolff, who took over Rowohlt's publishing house in Leipzig, and Wolff's representative during the early years of the war, Georg Heinrich Meyer, were far from unconditional admirers of Kafka, and they tended to drag their feet before sending some of the short stories to production; these texts appeared over the years in Kurt Wolff's series *Der jüngste Tag* (The day of judgment) or in his literary periodical *Die Weissen Blätter* (The white pages). Eight hundred to one thousand copies were usually printed, and reprints were rare. Already in early 1914 Kafka was considering leaving Wolff's publishing house for Samuel Fischer in Berlin, where Robert Musil, now an editor of the *Neue Rundschau*, was extending a most friendly invitation. Ultimately, nothing came out of these plans, and Kafka stayed with the Leipzig publisher.[35] Nonetheless, he became increasingly annoyed by Wolff's delays, and by 1918 he thought again of moving to another publisher.[36] When in 1922, after a long silence, Wolff wrote a mellifluously friendly letter to Kafka, asking for a new book, he didn't get it. Kafka's last volume of stories, *The Hunger Artist*, was published by Die Schmiede in Berlin and came out a few weeks after Kafka's death.

Joachim Unseld, who most thoroughly researched Kafka's publishing history, attributes the interruptions in his work and his inability to complete any of the three novels to the psychological impact of his lack of success with publishers, reviewers, and the reading public.[37] That was probably one factor among others.

3

In great part, Kafka's fiction was created independently from the literary revolution of his time and from modern literature more generally. This statement may at first seem absurd. For Milan Kundera, one of the major writers of our time, Kafka belongs "to the generation of the great innovators, Stravinski, Webern, Bartok, Apollinaire, Joyce, Picasso, Braque, all born like him between 1880 and 1883."[38] Yet Scott Spector, who, in his *Prague Territories* analyzed in depth Kafka's cultural and political milieu at the dawn of the twentieth century, is hesitant to link Kafka's writing with the modernist wave in Central and Western Europe to which Kundera alludes.[39]

In fact, Kafka was modern in one important aspect: in his rejection, in a later phase of writing, of the "ornaments" of fin-de-siècle literature and his mastery of a "sobriety" of style that has become one of the defining characteristics of his mature texts. Early on, as Anderson has shown, Kafka retained some of the aestheticism of his literary beginnings, still rooted in the Belle Époque: "Thus, while one can note an increased asceticism in Kafka's life and writing in this early period, the aestheticist impulse never entirely disappears."[40] The move toward "abstraction" does not become definitive before the end of 1912; it marks the turning point of Kafka's move from remnants of "ornament" toward an austere modernity.

Kafka's main literary references, on the other hand, belong to the nineteenth century, and his "circle"—Brod in particular—shared most of them.[41] Kafka didn't follow the radical changes in painting and music—he seems to have been uninterested in the visual arts and declared himself as being thoroughly unmusical. His antirepresentational literary approach was indeed adopted by modernist writers (and thinkers), but not until well after his death.

Of course, Kafka admired a number of his contemporaries, such as Robert Walser, Knut Hamsun, and, closer to home, Hugo von Hofmannstahl (and Karl Kraus!), but none of them can be considered as representative of the modernist literary wave. Robert Musil, whom Kafka knew and read, and who was considered as an exemplary modernist writer after the publication of *The Man without Qualities*, was the more traditional author of *The Confusions of Young Törless* during Kafka's lifetime.

There is, however, one major expression of modernist culture that Kafka avidly soaked in: the world of film. The first film theater opened in Prague in 1907.[42] In his earliest novel, *Amerika*, the memorable pursuit scene, in which Karl Rossmann flees from a policeman, clearly employs the acceleration techniques that were common in early silent films; for us, the passage unavoidably evokes Chaplin, though Kafka could not have seen his films when he wrote the novel.[43]

Many of the influences that Kafka himself alluded to have as much to do with the lives of the authors as with their writings. Thus, when the issue of marriage with Felice became acute, he wrote in one of his almost daily letters to her:

> Faced with your letters, faced by your pictures, I succumb. And yet—of the four men I consider to be my true blood-relations (without comparing myself to them either in power or in range) Grillparzer, Dostoevsky, Kleist and Flaubert, Dostoevsky was the only one to get married, and perhaps

Kleist, when compelled by outer and inner necessity to shoot himself on the Wannsee, was the only one to find the right solution. All this might be entirely irrelevant as far as we are concerned; after all, each of us lives life anew—even if I were standing in the very center of the shadow they cast upon our own time. But this is a fundamental question of life and faith in general, and from this point of view interpreting the behavior of these four men makes more sense.[44]

Of the four, the Austrian dramatist Franz Grillparzer may have impressed Kafka for no other reason than his renunciation to marriage to the woman he had fallen in love with and his finely crafted short story about it: "The Poor Musician" (*Der arme Spielmann*). He did not represent a literary influence, as Kafka himself admitted somewhat later.

There is, of course, no mystery about the impact of Dostoevsky's novels, in which psychological exploration moves from individual fate to fundamental metaphysical issues, a path that reflects and probably influenced Kafka's own probing. As we shall see, Dostoevsky may also have been at the origin of Kafka's own ironic version of "Redemption through Sin," in the words of Gershom Scholem, in his evocation of the self-sacrificing prostitute as a female saint and redeemer. Kafka was of course familiar with the role of Sonja in *Crime and Punishment*. This female character would reappear as Olga in *The Castle*.

As for Kleist, apart from the double suicide with his beloved, he represented such a central component of the most revered German literature that, for Kafka, his work—like that of Goethe—was part of the most fundamental literary heritage. A few texts in particular, Kleist's *Anekdoten* and the dialogue "On the Marionette Theater," may have had a significant influence on several of Kafka's short stories, on his aphorisms, and beyond.[45]

Kafka's frequently mentioned admiration for Flaubert probably derived first and foremost from the French novelist's extraordinary narrative style and his single-minded devotion to literary perfection. Thus in January 1913, he wrote to Felice: "I didn't have any blotting paper, and while waiting for the paper to dry, I read pages 600–602 of *Éducation*, which happened to be lying here. Dear God! Read that, dearest, do read it! '*Elle avoua qu'elle désirait faire un tour à son bras, dans les rues.*' What a sentence! What construction! Dearest, the pages on which so much is crossed out do not represent nights lacking in creative power. These are the very pages that absorbed him completely, in which he vanished from human sight. And even when writing it for the third time he experienced, as you can see in the appendix to this edition, that infinite happiness."[46]

One could add Strindberg and Tolstoy to the list and, regarding the second, some similarities between the Russian's *Diaries* and Kafka's aphorisms do appear.[47] Mainly, however, there was Kierkegaard: his life and his writings.

"Today," Kafka noted on August 21, 1913, "I got Kierkegaard's *Buch des Richters* [The book of the judge, in fact a selection from Kierkegaard's diaries]. As I suspected, his case, despite essential differences, is very similar to mine, at least he is on the same side of the world. He hears me out like a friend. I drafted the following letter to her father, which, if I have the strength, I will send off tomorrow."[48] The seeming non sequitur alludes to Kierkegaard's announcement to his fiancée, Regine Olsen, that he could not marry her; Kafka was about to send a letter in the same spirit to Felice's father.

Whether Kafka was already aware of it or not in 1913 or would recognize it only five years later, his life and that of the Danish philosopher and theologian had many more aspects in common, starting with difficult relations between father and son. Søren was twenty-five years old when, in August 1838, his eighty-two-year-old father died. Kierkegaard tore out some pages of his diary for 1843, but the surviving entries leave indications of the father's impact upon his own life that he claims influenced his rejection of Regine: "Had I explained myself [to Regine] I would have had to initiate her into the most frightful things, into my relationship with Father, his melancholia, the eternal night that broods deep within, my going astray, my lust and excesses . . ."[49] To this, a recent Kierkegaard biographer, Joakim Garff, adds: "The relationship to Regine was incompatible with the relationship to his father, who long after his death was still capable of warping his son's eros and hindering his ability to give himself. Kierkegaard could not explain this to Regine . . ."[50]

Later, in *Fear and Trembling*, Kierkegaard offered four versions of the biblical story of Abraham and Isaac on Mount Moriah. As Garff notes, in one version, Abraham "drew the knife before the text managed to supply him with a ram: If we count the number of times the various words occur, the biographical shudder is no less disturbing: In the four versions there appear, in all, four knives—versus only one ram! Do we have a better understanding of why, in his note to Boesen [the close friend to whom he sent a copy of *Fear and Trembling*] Kierkegaard signed himself as the *castrato* [singer] Farinelli?"[51]

In March 1918, Kafka wrote two major letters to Brod about Kierkegaard's ideas. During the preceding year, as well, the Danish thinker had been very much on Kafka's mind. Thus in October or November 1917, he wrote to Brod: "Kierkegaard is a star, although he shines over territory that is almost inaccessible to me. I'm glad that you will be reading him. I know only *Fear and Trembling* . . ."[52] Shortly thereafter, Kafka wrote again: "A few moments with a book (now it is Kierkegaard), toward evening a walk on the road, and this suffices me in my solitude."[53] In January 1918, in a letter about Oskar Baum that also mentioned Tolstoy, Kafka was somewhat more explicit:

Partly as a consequence of the visit [Baum] I started reading
Either/Or, with a special craving for help, the evening before
Oskar's departure, and am now reading Buber's most recent
books, sent by Oskar. Hateful, repellent books, all three of
them. To put it correctly and precisely, they are written—
Either/Or in particular—with the sharpest of pens . . . but
they drive you to despair. And as can happen when you are
reading passionately, you occasionally have the unconscious
feeling that they are the only books in the world, and even
the healthiest lungs feel out of breath. . . . They are books
that can be written as well as read only if one has at least a
trace of real superiority to them. As things are, their hateful-
ness grows under my hands.[54]

In another letter to Brod, Kafka mentioned the amount
owed to him by an Austrian paper for an unauthorized reprint-
ing of his short story "Report to an Academy": "The twenty
marks would be very welcome to me for, say, more Kierkegaard . . ."[55]

The two major letters Kafka addressed to Brod in March
1918 about Kierkegaard are manifestly part of their ongoing
discussion of the Danish thinker. They are the longest, most
intense, and most elaborate texts about any thinker or writer
Kafka ever mentioned. In mid-March, he explained why he
could not easily formulate in a letter what preoccupied him
at that moment. "I myself can do this simple thing only with
great effort, in contrast to the happily-unhappily transported
Kierkegaard, who so wonderfully steers the un-dirigible airship
even though to do so is not his primary concern. And to his
mind what is not a primary concern ought not be doable . . ."[56]

Apart from the personal similarities between their lives,
the impact of Kierkegaard's thinking on Kafka stems, first and
foremost, from the Danish philosopher's extraordinary insight
into the quintessence of the esthetic mode of being that, free
of all moral constraints, incessantly sought the victory of wan-

ton seduction followed by a no less triumphant rejection of the seduced other, of the destroyed other. The first part of Kierkegaard's *Either/Or* is mostly an analysis of various forms of seduction leading to its best-known chapter, "The Seducer's Diary." Yet Kafka may have found the clearest definition of his own method of seduction in chapter 2, "The Immediate Erotic Stages," in which Kierkegaard moves beyond Don Giovanni's erotic passion to Faust's spiritual seduction: "Faust, who is a reproduction of Don Giovanni, seduces only one girl, while Don Giovanni seduces hundreds; but then this one girl is, in terms of intensity, seduced and destroyed in quite another way from all those whom Don Giovanni has deceived. Simply because Faust, as a reproduction, has in him the category of spirit. The power of such a seducer is speech, that is to say, lies."[57]

For Kafka, the spoken "lies" used on chance feminine encounters became mostly written "lies" in his relations with Felice and Milena. Kafka seduced but knew of course from the outset that, at some point, the seduction would lead into a void, to an inescapable abandonment. Thus the question: were his attachments ever genuine? Did he see himself as a liar in the Kierkegaardian sense? How else to explain why *Either/Or* repelled him at first but why he felt compelled to reread it?

Beyond this crucial point, Kierkegaard's influence on Kafka stemmed most probably from the Dane's rejection of philosophical "systems" and the foundation of his philosophy upon individual experience, individual esthetic, or moral choice, on individual readiness to "the leap of faith," even if it appears as a rejection of basic moral commandments (*Fear and Trembling*). Kafka was never influenced by the Christian postulates of this earliest "existentialism," but embraced the fundamental dread and the lonely choices that belonged to the human condition as such.

"Kierkegaard's religious situation doesn't come across to me with the extraordinary clarity it has for you . . . ," Kafka wrote to Brod in the second of his long disquisitions of March 1918.

> . . . As he sees it, the relationship to the divine is primarily not subject to any outside judgment; perhaps this is so much so that Jesus himself would not be permitted to judge how far a follower of his has come. To Kierkegaard that seems to be more or less a question of the Last Judgment, which is to say answerable—in so far as an answer will be needed—only after the end of this world.
>
> Consequently the present external image of the religious relationship has no significance. Granted, the religious relationship wishes to reveal itself, but cannot do so in this world; therefore striving man must oppose this world in order to save the divine element within himself. Or what comes to the same thing, the divine sets him against the world to save itself . . .[58]

Immediately thereafter Kafka quotes Kierkegaard's lines about the man who is ready to defy the world in order to remain truthful to his own nature, whatever the world may demand.

Kafka's stand looks clear and coherent. And yet a few weeks before the letters about Kierkegaard, he had written the following aphorisms: "In the struggle between yourself and the world second the world." And he added: "One must not cheat anyone, not even the world of its victory."[59] At all levels of Kafka's writings contradictions are inherent to his way of thinking (or, more exactly, of dreaming), either as characteristic of the structure of dreams or as reflecting his constant struggle with the incompatible elements of the self.

4

The major political events that shook the world during Kafka's life left very few traces in his writings. One of his best-known diary entries is that of August 2, 1914: "Germany has declared war on Russia. Swimming in the afternoon."[60] As strange as it appears, the entry at least refers to the world scene. Usually there is no mention of it at all, although Kafka came of age after the collapse of traditional liberalism in the Austro-Hungarian Empire and during the exacerbation of nationalism and political antisemitism. He recorded none of this at the time. If Kafka had been in need of any justification, he could refer to a letter by Flaubert that he quoted in his diary in June 1912: "I have just read in Flaubert's letters: 'My novel is the cliff on which I am hanging, and I know nothing of what is going on in the world.'"[61]

After the war started, Kafka was mildly supportive of the imperial regime, expressing at times frustration about the incompetence of the Austro-Hungarian high command. Notoriously, he bought war bonds in 1915, probably expecting that German military prowess—which he admired—would achieve an ultimate victory. But all of this was fairly innocuous compared with his hatred of chauvinism and its public manifestations. He wrote of the noisy patriotic demonstrations of Prague Jewish businessmen, "German one day, Czech the next."[62] He went even farther in a strange entry at the very beginning of the war, on August 6, 1914: "I discover in myself nothing but pettiness, indecision, envy and hatred against those who are fighting and whom I passionately wish everything evil."[63] The outlook of this entry found no further expression during the war, and, as we have seen, at some point Kafka became actively involved in the care of disabled veterans.

In Kafka's diary and in his letters, one finds no mention of the assassinations of Archduke Franz Ferdinand and the French socialist leader Jean Jaurès, or of the major phases and events of the war and the immediate postwar years. The fall of the tsar and the Bolshevik Revolution, the American intervention in the European war, the armistices, the peace treaties, the disintegration of the Austro-Hungarian Empire, the establishment of the Czechoslovak Republic, the political rise of Thomas Masaryk—not a word appears in the diaries about any of these major developments. The peace agreements with Russia and the Ukraine are noted following Brod's cables about them, but nothing else until we reach the 1920s; even then, barely a few reactions surface, like the comments on "Munich" or on Walther Rathenau's assassination.

One must assume, of course, that Kafka discussed some of these events with his friends even though he didn't mention them in diaries or letters. Moreover, in mid-October 1918, he caught the Spanish influenza and thus was seriously ill during the crucial days that saw the end of the Dual Monarchy and the birth of Czechoslovakia. Nonetheless, the overall impression one gets from diaries and letters is that of indifference to world affairs and internal politics.

We owe the frequent mention of Kafka's supposed involvement in anarchism and socialism to Brod's "recollections" during the early 1930s; later on, Brod became less confident about his claims, though not before his assertions seeped into the literature about his friend.[64] Such political involvement would have been highly uncharacteristic, and Kafka never mentioned anything of the kind. But paradoxically, he did exhibit some interest about world affairs—albeit in a highly eccentric way: Kafka showed a keen and frequent fascination with accounts of military leadership, mostly those belonging to another epoch or to dreams.

The life of Alexander the Great and his battles came up on several occasions in the diaries and the blue octavo notebooks;[65] but Kafka's true hero was Napoleon. As a child Franz had already "wished to be brought face to face with the Emperor to show him how little effect he had. And, that was not courage, it was just coolness."[66] Later, Kafka's idolization of Napoleon grew. Thus in November 1911, Franz attended a lecture and recitation by the French poet and dramatist Jean Richepin: "La Légende de Napoléon": "I felt that Richepin had an effect upon me such as Solomon must have felt when he took young girls into his bed. I even had a slight vision of Napoleon who, in a connected fantasy, also stepped through the little entrance door. . . . He overwhelmed the entire hall, which was tightly packed at that moment. Near as I actually was to him, I had and would have had even in reality never a doubt of his effect . . ."[67] In October 1915, Kafka, having read volume 3 of Marcellin de Marbot's memoirs, presumably in the original French, analyzed in great detail Napoleon's Russian campaign.[68]

In letters and diary entries, Kafka delighted in quoting Napoleon's sayings and in imagining the emperor in surreal situations. The sayings, he admitted, had an emotional impact on him: "When I think of this anecdote—Napoleon is reminiscing at the royal table, at the royal court in Erfurt: 'When I was still a mere lieutenant in the Fifth Regiment' . . . (the royal highnesses look at each other in embarrassment, Napoleon notices it and corrects himself), 'When I still had the honor to be a mere lieutenant' . . . —the arteries of my neck swell with a pride that I can easily feel by identification and that has subtly penetrated in me."[69] On October 20: "Then leafed through 'Napoleon's maxims.' How easily you become for the moment a little part of your own tremendous notion of Napoleon!"[70] As for the surreal, in April 1921, Kafka writes to Brod about the disastrous relations with Milena; now (after their separation) a letter from Milena has arrived, asking him to give her some news: she promises not to answer. "She is unattainable for me," Kafka writes. "I must resign myself to that, and my energies are in such a state that they do so jubilantly. Which adds shame to the suffering; it is as if Napoleon had said to the demon that summoned him to Russia: 'I cannot go now: I haven't drunk my evening glass of milk yet'; and as if he then, when the demon asked, 'Will it take so long?' replied: 'Yes, I have to Fletcherize it.'"[71]

Had this cult for Napoleon been some sort of historical hobby, it wouldn't have amounted to much in Kafka's political imagination. It seems, however, that Napoleon was but the colorful object of a deeper longing for leadership that Kafka expressed in genuine, almost erotic emotion. Some of this impulse surfaces in the description of the German officer whom Kafka saw on the train, in Hungary, as he was accompanying his sister Elli on a visit to her husband stationed in Galicia: "The huge German officer, hung with every kind of equipment, marched first through the railway station, then through the train. His height and military bearing made him look stiff; it was almost surprising that he could move; the firmness of his waist, the breadth of his shoulders, the slimness of his body made one's eyes open wide in amazement in order to take it all in."[72]

A dream about the battle of the Tagliamento, recorded in November 1917, leaves the same impression. The battle is going badly for the Austrian side:

> Great despair, there will have to be a general retreat. A Prussian major appeared who had been watching the battle with us all the while; but when he calmly stepped forward into the suddenly deserted terrain, he seemed a new apparition. He put two fingers of each hand into his mouth and whistled the way one whistles a dog, though affectionately. This was a signal to his detachment, which had been waiting close by and now marched forward. They were Prussian Guards, silent young men, not many, perhaps only a company, all seemed to be officers, at least they carried long sabers and their uniforms were dark. When they marched by us, with short steps, slowly, in close order, now and then looking at us, the matter-of-factness of their death march was at once stirring, solemn and a promise of victory . . .[73]

Let us turn back to Kafka's most basic existential dilemma. In interpreting Kierkegaard, he had stressed the incompatibility of the divine (religious) in man with being part of this world. That was Kierkegaard. But, as Kafka didn't accept any religious commitment in the traditional sense, we may translate "religious" into "spiritual" or into the sacred fire of writing. In a roundabout way we face again the apparently insoluble contradiction of Kafka's life: he is a writer and nothing else; to write he needs an absolute separation from the world—a leap into the realm of the absolute from the domain of compromise, so to say—but he cannot live without the world, as the world also encompasses all the cravings and all the fears that are an integral part of his existence and his work. One is reminded of the drawing he sent to Milena: a torture machine that tears the victim apart down the middle of the body.

In referring to Kierkegaard's "leap of faith" that takes the biblical Abraham away from the moral norms of the world into a sphere of unconditional obedience to the call of God (sacrifice thy son Isaac, thy only son), Kafka describes another Abraham, one who would be ready for the terrifying transgression but cannot leave the world because of the daily, human tasks he must fulfill.

"I can imagine another Abraham," Kafka wrote to Robert Klopstock in June 1921, "who, to be sure, would not make it all the way to patriarch, not even to old clothes' dealer—who would be as ready to carry out the order for the sacrifice as a waiter would be ready to carry out his orders, but who would still never manage to perform the sacrifice because he cannot get away from home, he is indispensable, the farm needs him, there is always something he must attend to, the house isn't finished. But until the house is finished, until he has this security behind him, he cannot get away. The Bible perceives this too, for it says: 'He put his house in order.'"[74]

On one occasion, at least, Kafka appears to allude to some

synthesis, to some solution to his quandary, but this entry remains so enigmatic in its final line that any interpretation is possible: "I have vigorously absorbed the negative element of the age in which I live," Kafka wrote at the end of February 1918, "an age that is, of course, very close to me, which I have no right ever to fight against, but as it were a right to represent. The slight amount of the positive, and also of the extreme negative, which capsizes into the positive, are something in which I have had no hereditary share. I have not been guided into life by the hand of Christianity—admittedly now slack and failing—as Kierkegaard was, and have not caught the hem of the Jewish prayer shawl—now flying away from us—as the Zionists have . . ."

To this point, Kafka identifies with the world whose negative elements he has absorbed and that he feels the right to represent. Traditional religion (be it Christianity or Judaism) will be of no use in this representation. But might he be the carrier of a new spirituality that would grasp the essence of the age and be a guide for the future?

"I am," he writes, "an end or a beginning."[75]

6

An Ultimate Quest for Meaning?

AT TIMES KAFKA wrote with elation, even in an ecstatic mood, with a sense of quasi-mystical experience. On the day of his arrival on January 27, 1922, to Hotel Krone in Spindel-mühle, in yet another effort to improve his health, he noted: "The strange, mysterious, perhaps dangerous, perhaps saving comfort there is in writing. . . . A higher kind of observation is created, a higher, not a keener type and the higher it is . . . the more independent it becomes, the more obedient to its own laws of motion, the more incalculable, the more joyful, the more ascendant its course."[1]

A few months later, however, on July 5, a letter to Brod carried a different message: "Writing is a sweet and wonder-ful reward, but for what? In the night it became clear to me, as clear as a child's lesson book, that it is the reward for serving the devil. This descent to the dark powers, this unshackling of spirits bound by nature, these dubious embraces and whatever else may take place in the nether parts which the higher parts no longer know, when one writes one's stories in the sunshine. . . . Perhaps, there are other forms of writing, but I know only of this kind; at night, when fear keeps me from sleeping, I know only this kind. And the diabolic element in it seems very clear to me. It is vanity and sensuality . . ."[2]

This same letter started with the following lines: "Last night . . . what I had almost forgotten during the last relatively quiet time became clear to me: namely, on what frail ground or rather altogether nonexistent ground I live, over a darkness from which the dark power emerges when it wills and, heedless of my stammering, destroys my life . . ."[3]

The "dark power" could be the onset of depression, but given the "dubious embraces" that Kafka mentions later, and the "sensuality" that is one of the two diabolic elements that "buzz about one's own or even another's form—and feast on him,"[4] sexual urges seem more plausible. In his diary, he noted on June 5: "Bad days (G.). Already four or five days."[5] The "G." means *Geschlecht*, sex, and the entry is not included in Brod's edition.

During this period, Kafka was still sporadically working on *The Castle*. This third and final novel, which he started writing in the first person before changing his mind, appears occasionally like a personal legacy, as he knew that time was running short.[6]

I

During the months of 1920–1921 he spent at the Matliary sanatorium in the Tatra Mountains, Kafka's health did not improve (as it had not in Zürau or in Merano). Moreover, constant anxiety took its toll. In the diary entry of January 16, 1922, he explicitly mentioned a nervous breakdown and, a few days later, he described it to Brod.[7] In the same days, he noted: "I

fell asleep past midnight, awoke at five, a remarkable achievement for me, a remarkable good fortune; apart from that I still
felt sleepy. My good fortune, however, proved my misfortune,
or now the inevitable thought came: you don't deserve so much
good fortune; all the avenging furies flung themselves upon
me, I saw their enraged chieftain widely spread her fingers and
threaten me, or horribly strike cymbals . . ."[8]

When Kafka speaks of some streak of good fortune, of
some lucky break, the avenging furies cannot be very far. For
somebody as sensitive to the slightest noise as Kafka, the horrible striking of cymbals was an appropriate form of vengeance;
the spreading of the fingers, however, appears in a number of
texts, most memorably in *The Trial*, as Joseph K.'s own last gesture, before the executioners plunge the dagger into his heart.[9]

Notwithstanding brief moments of respite, despair remained the constant undertone. October 21, 1921: "All is imaginary—family, office, friends, the street, all imaginary, far away
or close at hand, the woman; the truth that lies closest, however, is only this, that you are beating your head against the wall
of a windowless and doorless cell."[10]

Such entombment was but another way of evoking Kafka's
worst fear: suffocating to death. In his diaries of that time,
suffocation appears in various guises: "Two children, alone in
their house," he wrote on December 6, 1921, "climbed into a
large trunk; the cover slammed shut, they could not open it,
and suffocated."[11] And, on December 20: "Undeniably, there is
a certain joy in being able calmly to write down: 'suffocation
is inconceivably horrible.' Of course it is inconceivable—that
is why I have written nothing down."[12] On January 31, 1922:
"For each invalid, his household god, for the tubercular the god
of suffocation."[13]

During the same months of 1922, particularly during the
first half of the year, as he was working on *The Castle*, Kafka,
according to his diaries, became haunted by his sexual needs, as

already briefly mentioned at the outset of the chapter. "What have you done with your gift of sex?" he noted on January 18. "It was a failure, in the end that is all that they will say." He then attempted to overcome his fear and his shame and to seize any occasion that might present itself: "Sex keeps gnawing at me," he continued, "hounds me day and night; I should have to conquer fear and shame and probably sorrow too to satisfy it; yet on the other hand I am certain that I should at once take advantage, with no feeling of fear or sorrow or shame, of the first opportunity to present itself quickly, close at hand, and willingly . . ."[14]

The new German edition indicates a prior entry on the same day (absent from the English version): "This is somewhat calmer," Kafka wrote, referring to the inner torture caused by the speeding of subjective time and alluding to his writing as an "assault on the last earthly frontier," described two days earlier; "instead of it comes sex. Salvation or worsening [of my situation] as one wishes."[15]

A few days later, Kafka will arrive in Spindelmühle. Soon thereafter the meeting with "little B." puts him to the test. It seems that Kafka chose "security" over "madness."

In February, Kafka returned to Prague, and in September 1922, he definitively abandoned his work on *The Castle*. In the meantime, at the Insurance Institute, he had been promoted to a significantly higher rank, which allowed him to retire in June that year with an adequate pension. During that summer in Plana (a small town where Ottla had rented a house), then during another stay of several months in Prague, Kafka completed a few short stories, including "A Hunger Artist," "A Married Couple," and "The Investigations of a Dog"; they would be followed, throughout 1923 and early 1924, by "The Burrow" and, finally, by "Josephine the Singer, or the Mouse Folk."

At the beginning of the summer of 1923, while vacationing in Müritz, a resort on the Baltic Sea, with his sister Elli and her family, Kafka met Dora Diamant, a twenty-five-year-old Jewish girl from an Orthodox Eastern European family who had left family and Orthodoxy to work with children in the Jewish People's Home in Berlin and now accompanied them to a summer camp located at the seaside, very close to Kafka's house. The two became acquainted at a Sabbath eve celebration at the Home—the first, Kafka wrote to Else Bergmann, that he had attended in his life.[16]

Franz and Dora soon decided to live together and, this time, Kafka took the decisive step: in September 1923, he left Prague and moved to Berlin with his companion. After a few months, however, life in Berlin (at a time of hyperinflation) became increasingly difficult and, as Franz's health steadily deteriorated, he and Dora had to move again. Brod had suggested that they settle in Schelesen, a small town near Prague, where Kafka had stayed in the early summer of 1923. Kafka responded in his usual ironic way, in January 1924: "If the creature were not so decrepit, you could almost make a drawing of his appearance: on the left D[ora], say, supporting him; on the right that man, say; some sort of 'scribbling' might stiffen his neck; now if only the ground beneath him were consolidated, the abyss in front of him filled in, the vultures around his head driven away, the storm in the skies above him quieted down—if all that were to happen, then it might be just barely possible to go on for a while . . ."[17]

In March 1924, Kafka, accompanied by Brod and Dora, returned to Prague. Barely two weeks later, the couple was again on its way, this time headed for Wienerwald, a sanatorium in lower Austria. By then, the infection had spread from the lungs to the larynx: "I had no chance to mention pneumothorax," Kafka wrote to Klopstock, on April 7. "Given my poor general condition (49 kilos in my winter clothes), it is out of the question. I have no contact with the rest of the place, lie in bed, also can only whisper (how quickly that went; just a touch of it started for the first time on about the third day in Prague)."[18] On April 13, Kafka informed Klopstock that he was being transferred to Professor Hajek's university clinic in Vienna: "It seems," he wrote, "my larynx is so swollen that I cannot eat; they must (they say) undertake alcohol injections into the nerve, probably also surgery."[19] On April 19, Kafka left Hajek's clinic for Dr. Hoffmann's sanatorium in Kierling near Klosterneuburg, where Robert joined Dora.

To avoid speaking, Kafka communicated most of the time by jotting on slips of paper. Any intake of food or medication was torture: "A little water; these bits of pills stick in the mucus like splinters of glass." Then: "If the noodles had not been so soft I couldn't have eaten them at all. Everything, even the beer burned me."[20]

Some two weeks before his death, Kafka received from Dora's Orthodox father a letter forbidding him to marry his daughter.[21] Kafka died on June 3, 1924, and was buried in the Jewish cemetery in Prague, Strašnice, on June 11. A week later, a memorial service at the Kleine Bühne (the Little Theater) in Prague, was attended by more than five hundred people: Kafka's fame was spreading.[22]

2

Although *The Trial* and *The Castle* were written eight years apart, the basic structure and the basic theme are very similar: an anonymous man—a bank official in *The Trial* and a land surveyor in *The Castle*—is "summoned" to fulfill a tragic destiny by an authority that he tries in vain to identify and to face.

Yet while *The Trial* is the story of an inexorable descent of the protagonist (Joseph K.) toward ultimate perdition, in *The Castle*, there are, at first glance, several episodes that could herald salvation for the protagonist (K.). And while in each novel, the main character is led astray by women, in *The Castle*, the main epiphanies are brought about by K.'s emotional or physical proximity to two males, Bürgel the castle official in the night scene described in chapter 3 and Hans Brunswick, the boy (inspired by little B. of the ski competition at the Tannenstein) who appears out of nowhere. Bürgel's explanations could guide K. on the path to his goal, but the land surveyor falls into deep sleep while the official chatters away. As for little Hans, who visits K. in secret to promise his help, he is but a young boy whose moral uprightness (he is incensed by the way K. is treated) and courage (he has slipped out of his classroom to meet K. and is risking punishment) may be as ephemeral as the innocence of childhood.

I just mentioned that in both *The Trial* and in *The Castle*, the protagonist is led astray by women. As we saw in chapter 3, Ritchie Robertson reached the same conclusion about Karl Rossmann's fate in *Amerika*, and Klaus Wagenbach pointed to the whorish characteristics of women in the last two novels. In this context, what could Kafka have meant by setting at center stage in *The Castle* two sisters, Amalia and Olga, who, along with their family, are excluded from the village community precisely because one of them, beautiful Amalia, has rejected the lewd advances of a castle official? The official, Sortini, sees Amalia at a village festivity—where he represented the castle—and the next day sends her a letter that quite unequivocally invites her into his bed. Amalia tears the letter to pieces and throws them at the face of the servant who brought it.

Amalia's story, as told at length by Olga, could mean, of course, that even in our earthly, ordinary world (the village in the novel) there are exceptional characters who keep their dignity in the most trying circumstances. Sortini is not seen again and no official complaint is lodged, but twice a week Olga spends the night with the castle's servants in the stable of the Gentlemen's Inn in order to find the one who brought the offensive letter to Amalia, in the hope of begging his pardon thus redeeming her family. As I mentioned, Olga may have had a literary model: Sonja in *Crime and Punishment*, who chooses prostitution to save her family ruined by the father, the drunkard Marmeladov.

Of course, Kafka never hinted at the meaning of the episode of the two sisters, but a closer look shows that the sisters are consistent with his representation of women. The marmorean Amalia keeps away from any contact—she hardly speaks to K.—and proves immune to sexual advances: she is not threatening, she is not a typical female anymore. Olga is a warm and generous soul, but still a whore for more than two years, as she admits to K. Kafka's irony is obvious: Olga is no Sonja, and her seeming attraction to K. intimates potential danger. Thus little Hans remains the only—if uncertain and far-off—portent of salvation. What Kafka had in mind about the future role of the boy whom he described lovingly and at great length we do not know.

In fact, the novel doesn't lack indications of K.'s ultimate downfall. One of the most explicit of such signs follows K.'s attempt to speak to Klamm, the castle official who appears to be in charge of his case and whom K. has seen only once— asleep—through a keyhole. K. literally lays in wait at night in the courtyard of the Gentlemen's Inn, as Klamm, whose coach stands ready, is expected to come out at any moment to return to the castle. But, probably forewarned, Klamm doesn't appear, the horse is unharnessed, the coachman leaves, and K.—for whom the courtyard is off-limits—remains alone. "It seemed to K. as if they had broken off all contact with him, but as if he were freer than ever and could wait as long as he wanted here in this place where he was generally not allowed, and as if he had fought for this freedom for himself in a manner nobody else could have done and as if nobody could touch him or drive him away, or even speak to him, yet—and this conviction was at least equally strong—as if there were nothing more senseless, nothing more desperate, than this freedom, this waiting, this invulnerability."[23]

What meaning did Kafka attribute to this "senseless freedom"? Did it confirm the uselessness of all hope? As we saw, Kafka wrote *The Castle* at a time of deepest personal crisis, tormented by recurrent fits of depression, by terrifying imaginings, by the impossibility of satisfying his sexual cravings out of "fear" and "shame." Wasn't it enough to convince him that whatever measure of freedom was given, it was senseless? Moreover, he knew that even the most refined exegesis couldn't offer any answer about the significance, even the nature of freedom. In December 1917, in one of his aphorisms, he had written: "For everything outside the phenomenal world, language can only be used allusively, but never even approximately in a comparative way, since, corresponding as it does to the phenomenal world, it is concerned only with property and its relations."[24]

Otherwise put: You are free, but abandon all hope to understand the meaning of that freedom. You don't have the language and the notions that would allow you to accede to the realm of freedom. Kafka became even more emphatic in the story he started immediately after leaving aside *The Castle:* "The Investigations of a Dog."

"Investigations" tells of an old, wise, and scientifically inclined dog who attempts by empirical means, theoretical reasoning, and the examination of many possible viewpoints to understand diverse aspects of "doghood": to explore various unexpected, at times scandalous, modes of canine behavior and — this is his main aim — to discover the provenance of dogs' food. This wise dog's subtle reasoning exhibits only one blind spot: the inability to recognize the existence of humans. This charming and witty story is not an attempt to set up a Kantian *Critique* for dogs; Kafka points to the limits of human understanding, to our inability to perceive some dimensions of our existence.

Is Kafka thereby repudiating his previous forays into a spiritual world, his "quest for meaning" that most commentators have attributed to the "Aphorisms," to *The Castle*, and to the later stories? The quest may not have been abandoned, but it appears to have become increasingly open-ended, increasingly skeptical, maybe even increasingly disenchanted and ironic.

We have seen that Kafka was indifferent to Judaism as religious faith or practice. Whether during the last years of his life he followed less religiously defined spiritual paths we do not know; we know, however, that neither in his correspondence nor in his diaries did he refer explicitly to anything of the kind.

One may also read the "Investigations" as a belated commentary on Kafka's prior writings, an indirect interpretation of *The Castle* and *The Trial*, among other texts. The dog cannot take into account a dimension he is unable to see, and thus he misunderstands the most important issues of "doghood." In a somewhat similar way, the inhabitants of the village (K. among them) cannot grasp the essence, the function, and the meaning of the castle. The teacher whom K. meets at the outset of the novel is shocked when asked whether he knows Count West-west, the supposed master of the castle. Does the count exist at all? Do the superior judges exist in *The Trial*? Is the Law real? The "man from the country" who waits before the door of the Law sees only a light coming from what is supposed to be the domain of the Law. Who knows whether this light has its source in the Law, whether it is a radiance emitted by the Law, or is merely the visual illusion of an old man about to die. Eric Santner has nuanced the possible nonexistence of the Law: "[The] master's discourse [that implies the presence of the law] . . . has been attenuated and dispersed across a field of relays and points of contact that no longer cohere, even in fantasy, as a consistent 'other' of possible address and redress. In Kafka, the law is everywhere and nowhere."[25]

In *The Castle*, we know practically nothing about the domain of men—that is, about the castle as such. Contrarily, we know more than we need about that moral swamp, the village, dominated by its women. Whereas in Kafka's ironic fantasy, the castle may symbolize some form of perverse spirituality—its manifestations are merely sexual and predatory—the village, in its concrete abjection, appears at times as a reflection of Kafka's personal wanderings from one disastrous relation with women to the next, haunted by a desire he cannot satisfy.

3

In Kafka's fiction all main characters, humans or animals, try to reach some unattainable goal, and all such hopes are dashed. As in Genesis, where an angel with flaming sword stands guard at the gate of Paradise, thus in Kafka's fiction the possibility of entering (or returning to) some land imagined as free and promised is blocked by insuperable obstacles. But whereas in Genesis it is the God of the Bible who forbids the return to Paradise after the Fall, in Kafka's texts we, like the protagonists, never find out what power crushes such fundamental human hope, the symbolic sum total of all human hopes.

Is there no exception? Isn't Kafka's first novel, *Amerika*, a tale of Fall and Redemption? After being the innocent victim of one expulsion after another (from family and homeland, from his American uncle's house, from the Pollunder house, from Hotel Occidental) and spiraling down to become servant in a brothel, doesn't young Karl Rossmann, when setting foot on the Clayton racecourse and entering the great Oklahoma Theater, find paradise? Every applicant is hired, angels on pedestals blow trumpets; it all looks miraculous. According to Brod, Kafka had indeed mentioned some sort of surreal finale to the novel, including a reunion of Karl with his parents. If Brod's reminiscences are correct, then the chance is that Kafka was gently pulling his leg.

The great Oklahoma Theater is a perfect illustration of Kafka's ironic representation of a fake paradise: the "Amerika" that immigrants and other Europeans were dreaming of. The Oklahoma Theater appears clearly as unadulterated kitsch, but kitsch with threatening undertones. On the train taking them to some unknown destination, the passengers, all newly hired by the theater—Karl among them—rush through a landscape more ominous than soothing, an intimation more of hell than of paradise, as the last sentence of the novel hints at: dark mountains, rushing streams that "plunged under the bridges over which the train passed, so close that the chill breath of them made their faces shudder."[26]

Such an interpretation, albeit close to what seemed to be Kafka's view, runs nonetheless counter to two major aphorisms written at the end of 1917; first, "Man cannot live without a permanent trust in something indestructible in himself, though both the indestructible element and the trust may remain permanently hidden from him."[27] And, even more pointed: "There is nothing besides a spiritual world; what we call the world of the senses is the evil in the spiritual world, and what we call Evil is only the necessity of a moment in our eternal evolution."[28]

As we saw, Brod attempted to overcome the contradiction between Kafka's fiction and the aphorisms by considering them as carrying two entirely different worldviews.[29] The difficulty with Brod's attempts has been highlighted throughout this book; moreover, it cannot explain Kafka's writing of his most desperate texts after the bulk of the aphorisms had been completed or, in particular, the contradictory message of the aphorisms as such. As the priest in the Cathedral scene in *The Trial* tells K.: "The right perception of any matter and a misunderstanding of the same matter do not wholly exclude each other."[30]

"What we call Evil is only the necessity of a moment in our eternal evolution": in that second clause of the aphorism, the key word is not "Evil," as its nature is wrapped in uncertainty ("what we call Evil"); the key word is "necessity," a concept that carries its inherent finality. It sends us back to the closing moments of the debate between Joseph K. and the priest. To counter one of the accused's final arguments, the priest answers: "No, . . . it is not necessary to accept everything as true, one must only accept it as necessary." A statement that leads to Joseph K.'s despondent answer: "A melancholy conclusion, . . . It turns lying into a universal principle."[31]

It does more. "Necessity" haphazardly determines the moment during which Evil will reign "in our eternal evolution." "Necessity" is the supreme force of Greek mythology; it is *Ananké* or "Fate": it rules over gods and men. Kafka knew his Greek mythology well, as several of his stories indicate and as the classical education of his high school days would have instilled in him in any case. The evil demiurge of Gnosticism may have been on his mind, but it was more plausibly Ananké, blind fate, that indifferently plays with the lives of human beings. It could be both: Fate haphazardly chooses the victims; the evil demiurge follows up in outlining the course of their downfall.

If, however, Kafka's world is dominated by the eventually catastrophic vagaries of blind fate and by the forces of evil, what can be the writer's role? Why write? Why the need to create? At the end of 1917, as we have seen, Kafka still harbored the faint hope that his writing could "raise the world into the pure, the true and the immutable." Over time, he increasingly considered his writing as "the reward for serving the devil." And yet, as he noted in his ultimate diary entry, on June 12, 1923, although every word he wrote was "twisted in the hands of the spirits" and became "a spear turned against the speaker," he knew that for him, writing remained his only defense: "more than consolation is: You too have weapons."[32]

Weapons against Fate? Kafka had no such naïve expectations. Actually, in his late stories he seems to try, repeatedly, to answer the paradox of artistic creation in an aimless world and for an aimless humanity. In "The Burrow" and "A Hunger Artist," the conclusion appears to be clear: creation is an obsessive need, an all-consuming passion bound to fail, or, more precisely, incapable of leading to any desirable or useful result. The animal who digs a perfect underground labyrinth for his security and accumulates mounds of food for indefinite survival in his fortress knows that his sense of security is deceptive: "The most beautiful thing about my burrow is the stillness. Of course, that is deceptive. At any moment it may be shattered and then all will be over . . ."[33] In this story which remained unfinished, the reason for going on is offered at the outset: "All this involves very laborious calculation, and the sheer pleasure of the mind in its own keenness is often the sole reason why one keeps it up."[34] This is Kafka's own voice, and the ultimate failure of the animal to hide is unavoidable in Kafka's world.

In many ways, "A Hunger Artist," written at the same time as *The Castle*, is more desperate: the extraordinary fast of the artist, a fast that lasts longer than any set goal, bores the crowd, which soon also accuses him of cheating: "And when once in a while some leisurely passerby stopped, made merry over the old figure on the board, and spoke of swindling, that was in its way the stupidest lie ever invented by indifference and inborn malice, since it was not the hunger artist who was cheating, he was working honestly, but the world was cheating him of his reward."[35]

Kafka's attitude mellowed in his last story, "Josephine the Singer, or the Mouse Folk," the proofs of which he corrected during the terminal stage of his illness. The writer becomes an essential element of a community under threat (there is always a possibility of threat against the community of mice, the Jewish Folk, but there is also an inexorable threat inherent in every human existence: the vagaries of Fate and ultimately death). Josephine the Singer is a mouse like any mouse, but one who believes in her unique talent and behaves as imperiously as any diva. She draws crowds of mice to her performances, although most of the mice have long recognized that her singing is no different from ordinary piping. But the folk need to assemble around Josephine, they need "somebody making a ceremonial performance out of doing the usual thing."[36]

The final lines of "Josephine the Singer" are marked by an elegiac tone, unusual in Kafka's stories; it conveys resignation, as if weapons couldn't help anymore, as if the writer's limited role was to provide the community with a temporary illusion, necessary but ephemeral, a mere "ceremonial performance," itself ultimately destroyed—like Franz Kafka's own life.

NOTES

Epigraph: Letter from Siegfried Wolff to Franz Kafka, April 10, 1917, Marbacher Facsimile 43, *Deutsche Schillergesellschaft*, Marbach 2002, my translation.

Introduction

1. Fyodor Dostoevsky, *The Brothers Karamazov* (New York, 2004), 123.

2. Franz Kafka, *The Castle* (New York, 1998), 1; hereafter *C*.

3. See Hartmut Binder, *Kafka Kommentar zu den Romanen, Rezensionen, Aphorismen und zum Brief an den Vater* (Munich, 1976), 279.

4. Erich Heller, *Franz Kafka* (New York, 1974), ix.

5. Ibid.

6. Franz Kafka, *The Diaries, 1910–1923* (New York, 1976), 423; hereafter *D*.

7. Max Brod, *Franz Kafka, Eine Freundschaft*, vol. 2, *Brief-wechsel*, ed. Malcolm Pasley (Frankfurt, 1989), 228.

8. Franz Kafka, *Letters to Friends, Family, and Editors* (New York, 1977), 200; hereafter *LFr*.

9. George Steiner, Introduction to Franz Kafka, *The Trial* (New York, 1992), xi; hereafter *T*.

10. John Updike, Foreword to Franz Kafka, *The Complete Stories*, ed. Nahum N. Glatzer (New York, 1971), ix; hereafter *CS*.

11. On this aspect see Walter Sokel, "K. as Imposter: His Quest for Meaning," in *Twentieth Century Interpretations of "The Castle*," ed. Peter F. Neumeyer (Englewood Cliffs, NJ, 1969), 32–35.

12. On this important issue see Mark M. Anderson, *Kafka's Clothes: Ornament and Aestheticism in the Habsburg Fin de Siècle* (Oxford, 1992), 55n5.

13. Brod attempted to explain away some "slight omissions" from the letters and the diaries as meant to protect the privacy of persons still alive. See Max Brod, *Streitbares Leben, 1884–1968* (Munich, 1969), 191.

14. Jacques Derrida, "Préjugés, devant la loi," in Jacques Derrida et al., *La Faculté de juger* (Paris, 1985), 127.

15. Franz Kafka, *Letters to Milena* (New York, 1990), 169; hereafter *LM*.

16. Mark M. Anderson, "Kafka, Homosexuality, and the Aesthetics of Male Culture," in *Gender and Politics in Austrian Fiction*, ed. Ritchie Robertson and Edward Timms (Edinburgh, 1996), 79–99.

17. See for example Thomas Karlauf, *Stefan George. Die Entdeckung des Charisma* (Munich, 2007), 69–71. Also, Hermann Kurzke, *Thomas Mann, Das Leben als Kuntstwerk* (Munich, 1999), 50–55.

18. *D*, 410–411.

19. *T*, 229.

20. *D*, 343–344.

21. Ibid., 423.

22. Richard Ellmann, *James Joyce* (Oxford, 1983), 5.

23. Erich Heller, *Thomas Mann: The Ironic German* (1958; Cambridge, 1981).

24. *D*, 394.

Part I. "Prague Doesn't Let Go . . . "

Title from Franz Kafka to Oskar Pollak, December 20, 1902, *LFr*, 5.

1. The Son

1. *LFr*, 294–297.

2. Stéphane Moses, *Exégèse d'une Légende. Lectures de Kafka* (Paris, 2006), 67–70.

3. For the historical background, see essentially Christoph Stölzl, *Kafkas böses Böhmen: Zur Sozialgeschichte eines Prager Juden* (Munich, 1975), and Hillel J. Kieval, *Languages of Community: The Jewish Experience in the Czech Lands* (Berkeley, 2000).

4. Franz Kafka, *Briefe*, vol. 1, *1900–1912* (Frankfurt, 1999), 111.

5. *LFr*, 42.

6. *D*, 365.

7. Franz Kafka, *The Metamorphosis*, trans. and ed. Stanley Corngold (New York, 1996), 26.

8. Ibid., 29.

9. Ibid.

10. Franz Kafka, "Letter to His Father," in *The Sons* (New York, 1989), 132–133.

11. Ibid., 115–167.

12. For a different perception of Hermann Kafka, see František X. Bašik, "Als Lehrjunge in der Galanteriewarenhandlung Hermann Kafka," in *Franz Kafka, Brief an den Vater*, ed. Hans-Gerd Koch (Berlin, 2004), 69–130. For another reevaluation of Hermann's personality see also Alena Wagnerová, "Der Bürger der königlichen Haupstadt Prag Hermann Kafka und seine Familie," ibid., 131–139.

13. Kafka, "Letter to His Father," 120–121.

14. Ibid., 130–131.

15. *LFr*, 201.

16. *D*, 59.

17. Klaus Wagenbach, *Kafka* (Cambridge, 2003), 12.

18. *LFr*, 414.

19. For a masterful interpretation of this transformation in Austria, see Carl E. Schorske, *Fin-de-Siècle Vienna: Politics and Culture* (New York, 1981).

20. *D*, 171.

21. Franz Kafka, *Lettres à Ottla* (Paris, 1978), 40–41.

22. Ibid., 56–59. Franz had directly expressed this point in a letter to both his parents, in July 1914, as he thought of moving to Berlin; ibid., 28–30.

23. Kafka, "Letter to His Father," 150.

24. Ibid., 167.

25. *CS*, 84.

26. Ibid.

27. Kafka, *The Metamorphosis*, 27–28; translation slightly altered.

28. Ibid., 28.

29. Kafka, "Letter to his Father," 163.

30. Eric Santner, "Kafka's *Metamorphosis* and the Writing of Abjection" in Kafka, *The Metamorphosis*, 197.

31. Kafka, *The Metamorphosis*, 40–41.

32. Ibid., 3.

33. *T*, 29.

34. Kafka, *The Metamorphosis*, 36.

35. Ibid., 38.

36. See, for the text, Kafka, *The Metamorphosis*, 3; for Corngold's comment, see ibid., 87.

37. *CS*, 88.

38. Kafka, *The Metamorphosis*, 39.

39. *CS*, 167.

40. Peter-André Alt, *Franz Kafka. Der ewige Sohn* (Munich, 2005), 15.

2. "The Dark Complexity of Judaism"

1. *LM,* 19.

2. Quoted in Dominique Schnapper, "Intégration et cito-yenneté: Le modèle français," in *Les Juifs et le XXe siècle. Dictionnaire critique,* ed. Elie Barnavi and Saul Friedländer (Paris, 2000), 380.

3. Arthur Schnitzler, *The Road into the Open,* trans. Roger Byers (Berkeley, 1992). Kafka disliked Schnitzler's writings.

4. Anthony Northey, *Kafka's Relatives: Their Lives and His Writing* (New Haven, 1991), 85.

5. Kafka, "Letter to His Father," 146.

6. Ibid., 147-148.

7. *LFr,* 289.

8. Ibid., 10.

9. Franz Kafka, *Reisetagebücher,* ed. Hans-Gerd Koch et al. (Frankfurt, 1994), 27, 38.

10. *D,* 64-66.

11. Kafka, "Letter to His Father," 123.

12. *D,* 181-182 ("My parents were not there," Kafka noted). For the full text of the lecture, see Franz Kafka, *Beschreibung eines Kampfes und andere Schriften aus dem Nachlass* (Frankfurt, 2004), 149-153.

13. *LFr,* 283.

14. Ibid., 150.

15. Sander Gilman, *Franz Kafka: The Jewish Patient* (New York, 1995), 39.

16. Otto Weininger, *Geschlecht und Charakter: Eine prinzipielle Untersuchung* (1903; Munich, 1980). English translation: *Sex and Character,* n.d.

17. Chandak Sangoopta, *Otto Weininger: Sex, Science, and Self in Imperial Vienna* (Chicago, 2000), 1.

18. Ibid., 19-20.

19. *LFr,* 276.

20. See, for example, the harshly ironic article entitled "The Jewish Patient" published in March 1914 in the Prague Zion-

ist Journal *Selbstwehr*, which Kafka read assiduously. Quoted in Gilman, *Franz Kafka*, 64.

21. *LM*, 46.

22. *D*, 252.

23. *LFr*, 236.

24. Ibid., 289.

25. Franz Kafka, *Letters to Felice*, ed. Erich Heller and Jürgen Born (New York, 1973), 517; hereafter *LF*.

26. *D*, 152.

27. Ibid., 98–99.

28. Ibid., 172.

29. Ibid., 173–176.

30. *LF*, 157.

31. Ibid., 164.

32. *LFr*, 147.

33. Ibid., 122.

34. *LF*, 500.

35. Ibid., 502–503.

36. Ibid., 185–186.

37. *LFr*, 347.

38. *LM*, 51.

39. For a summary see Ritchie Robertson, *Kafka: Judaism, Politics, and Literature* (Oxford, 1985), 12. Among the most thorough attempts at such a linkage, see Arnold Band, "The Beilis Trial in Literature: Notes on History and Fiction," in *Studies in Modern Jewish Literature* (Philadelphia, 2003), 33–50.

40. *LM*, 212–213.

41. *LFr*, 328.

42. *LM*, 51.

43. About the Zionist scene in Prague and Kafka's involvement, see in particular Iris Bruce, *Kafka and Cultural Zionism* (Madison, WI, 2007).

44. For a thorough description of this campaign, see Giuliano Baioni, *Kafka. Literatur und Judentum* (Stuttgart, 1994), 109 ff.

45. See in particular Leo A. Lensing, "Fackel-Leser und Werfel-Verehrer. Anmerkungen zu Kafka Briefen an Robert Klop-

stock," in *Kafkas letzter Freund*, ed. Hugo Wetscherek (Vienna, 2003), 267 ff.

46. No less misleading in this respect are Hugo Bergmann's reminiscences. See Hugo Bergmann, "Schulzeit und Studium," in *"Als Kafka mir entgegenkam . . ." Erinnerungen an Franz Kafka*, ed. Hans-Gerd Koch (Berlin, 1995), 22–23.

47. *LF*, 423.

48. Ibid., 501.

49. Hartmut Binder, "Franz Kafka and the Weekly Paper 'Selbstwehr,'" *Leo Baeck Institute Yearbook* 12 (1967), 139 ff.

50. About this visit, see Hans Zieschler, *Kafka geht ins Kino* (Reinbek bei Hamburg, 1996), 145.

51. For a summary on this issue, see Bruce, *Kafka and Cultural Zionism*, 165 ff, 179 ff.

52. *LFr*, 388.

53. Bruce, *Kafka and Cultural Zionism*, 182.

54. *LFr*, 373–374.

55. *LM*, 236.

56. Kafka, *Lettres à Ottla*, 76–77.

57. Franz Kafka, *Das Ehepaar und andere Schriften aus dem Nachlass* (Frankfurt, 1992), 35.

58. Ibid., 35–36.

59. Updike, Foreword to *CS*, xx.

60. Hannah Arendt, *The Jewish Writings*, ed. Jerome Kohn and Ron H. Feldman (New York, 2007), 290.

61. For a closely argued philosophical analysis of Benjamin's interpretation of Kafka, see most recently Eli Friedlander, *Walter Benjamin: A Philosophical Portrait* (Cambridge, MA, 2012), 212–220.

62. Moshe Idel, *Old Worlds, New Mirrors: On Jewish Mysticism and Twentieth Century Thought* (Philadelphia, 2010), 118–119.

63. Walter Benjamin, "Franz Kafka: On the Tenth Anniversary of His Death," in *Walter Benjamin: Selected Writings*, vol. 2, *1927–1934*, ed. Michael Jennings (Cambridge, MA, 1999), 794–818.

64. Walter Benjamin, "Letter to Gershom Scholem on Franz Kafka," in *Walter Benjamin: Selected Writings*, vol. 3, *1935–1938*, ed.

Howard Eiland and Michael W. Jennings (Cambridge, MA, 2002), 322–329.

65. For this translation, see Walter Benjamin, *Illuminations: Essays and Reflections*, ed. Hannah Arendt (New York, 1968), 143–145.

66. Reiner Stach, *Kafka. Die Jahre der Erkenntnis* (Frankfurt, 2002), 255.

67. Franz Kafka, *The Blue Octavo Notebooks*, ed. Max Brod (Cambridge, 1991), 28; hereafter *BON*.

3. Love, Sex, and Fantasies

1. For the entire photograph and a few details about Hansi, see Alt, *Franz Kafka*, 181. As for the typical dust-jacket picture, see, for example, Wagenbach, *Kafka*, or the frontispiece of this book.

2. Anderson, "Kafka, Homosexuality, and Aesthetics," 79–82.

3. Kafka, *Briefe*, 1: 53; the English translation has been partly censored, following Brod's edition.

4. *D*, 207.

5. Ibid., 362.

6. Ibid., 228.

7. Franz Kafka, *Tagebücher Band III, 1914–1923*, ed. Hans-Gerd Koch et al. (Frankfurt, 1994), 131; hereafter *TgbIII*. For some mysterious reason, Brod considered the exclusion of this sentence necessary.

8. Elias Canetti, *Kafka's Other Trial: The Letters to Felice* (New York, 1974).

9. *LFr*, 109.

10. *TgbIII*, 288.

11. *LM*, 247–248.

12. Ibid., 249.

13. Ibid., 147.

14. Ibid.

15. Ibid., 147–148.

16. Ibid., 161.

17. *LFr*, 273.

18. Ibid., 194.

19. *D*, 59.

20. Franz Kafka, *Tagebücher Band I, 1909–1912*, ed. Hans-Gerd Koch et al. (Frankfurt, 1994), 41; hereafter *TgbI*.

21. Ibid., 290.

22. *D*, 59.

23. *LFr*, 45.

24. Kafka, *Reisetagebücher*, 41.

25. *D*, 459.

26. Ibid., 238.

27. *TgbIII*, 288.

28. *CS*, 55–56.

29. Wagenbach, *Kafka*, 86.

30. Robertson, *Kafka, Judaism, Politics*, 72.

31. Reiner Stach, *Kafkas erotischer Mythos: Eine ästhetische Konstruktion des Weiblichen* (Frankfurt, 1987); Elisabeth Boa, *Kafka: Gender, Class, and Race in the Letters and Fictions* (Oxford, 1996).

32. *T*, 225–226.

33. *TgbI*, 214.

34. Kafka, *Reisetagebücher*, 11.

35. Hugo Hecht, "Zwölf Jahre in der Schule mit Franz Kafka," in Koch, *"Als Kafka mir entgegenkam . . . ,"* 33.

36. *LFr*, 2; *Briefe, 1902–1924*, ed. Max Brod and Klaus Wagenbach (Frankfurt, 1975), 10, 11.

37. *LF*, 179.

38. *D*, 267.

39. *LFr*, 167.

40. *D*, 172.

41. Kafka, *Reisetagebücher*, 101. The Brod version keeps only the sentence ending with "Schiller." *D*, 481.

42. *TgbI*, 75.

43. *LFr*, 274.

44. Ibid., 307.

45. *D*, 403.

46. Franz Kafka, *Journal* (1954; Paris, 2002), 552.

47. *D*, 478. The English translation of Kafka's *Diaries* comprises the "Travel Diaries," also censored by Brod.

48. Kafka, *Reisetagebücher*, 96.

49. *D*, 410–411; bracketed passages were deleted by Brod.

50. Ibid., 411.

51. I am grateful to Amir Kenan for reminding me of Lewis Carroll.

52. Kafka, *Reisetagebücher*, 103.

53. "Der Aufstieg im 'stillen Tal'": for the translated part, see *D*, 227; for the nontranslated sentence, Franz Kafka, *Tagebücher Band II, 1912–1914*, ed. Hans-Gerd Koch et al. (Frankfurt, 1994), 187; hereafter *TgbII*.

54. *D*, 113.

55. *CS*, 49–51.

56. Franz Kafka, *Beschreibung eines Kampfes und andere Schriften aus dem Nachlass* (Frankfurt, 1994), 133.

57. Anderson, *Kafka's Clothes*, 49.

58. Heinz Politzer, *Franz Kafka: Parable and Paradox* (Ithaca, NY, 1966), 255.

59. *C*, 265.

60. Ibid.

61. Ibid., 270.

62. *CS*, 411–412.

63. Ibid., 213.

64. *D*, 357–360.

65. Anderson, "Kafka, Homosexuality, and Aesthetics," 96.

66. Dagmar C. G. Lorenz, "Kafka and Gender," in *The Cambridge Companion to Kafka*, ed. Julian Preece (Cambridge, 2003), 175. On the other hand, it appears at times (although such a remark sounds almost absurd regarding a text by Kafka) that too much may be read into some passages. The Stoker scene is generally interpreted as a homosexual allusion, but to consider "Uncle Jacob" and Pollunder as "mildly homosexual" may not be as convincing. For this interpretation see Robertson, *Kafka*, 70.

67. Reiner Stach, *Kafka: Die Jahre der Entscheidungen* (Frankfurt, 2002), 560–561.

68. *LM*, 216.

69. *CS*, 442–443.

70. *D*, 224.

71. Ibid., 221.

72. Ibid., 342.

73. Ibid., 101.

74. *CS*, 166.

75. *LFr*, 95.

76. *D*, 226.

77. Ibid., 310.

78. Ibid., 357.

79. *LM*, 204–205.

80. *T*, 193–194.

81. Ibid., 196.

82. Ibid., 84.

83. Ibid., 85.

84. Ibid., 88.

85. Ibid., 89.

86. Franz Kafka, *Beim Bau der chinesischen Mauer und andere Schriften aus dem Nachlass* (Frankfurt, 2006), 117.

87. *D*, 412–413.

88. Ibid., 412.

Part II. "The Reward for Serving the Devil"

Title from Franz Kafka to Max Brod, July 5, 1922, *LFr*, 333.

4. Night Journey

1. *D*, 386–387. For the dating of "A Country Doctor," see Hartmut Binder, *Kafka—Kommentar zu sämtlichen Erzählungen* (Munich, 1975), 208.

2. *CS*, 220.

3. Ibid., 221.

4. Ibid., 220.

5. Ibid., 222, 223.

6. Ibid.

7. Ibid.

8. Alt, *Franz Kafka*, 505–506.

9. Ibid., 224.

10. Ibid.

11. *D*, 362.

12. *CS*, 225.

13. One could of course add King Lear's "Howl, howl, howl, howl!" But while there is no indication of Kafka's having read Shakespeare beyond *Hamlet* and *Richard III*, there is a distinct possibility that he knew Conrad's text. Kafka was interested in his maternal uncle Joseph Löwy's railway building career in the Congo, and the author evokes "Middle Congo" (*Mittleren Kongo*) in his octavo notebooks. According to Anthony Northey, "Memoirs of the Kalda Railway" were directly influenced by the uncle's activities. See Northey, *Kafka's Relatives*, 15–25, particularly 18–25.

14. For this summary of the story, see Baioni, *Kafka*, 142.

15. For this legend, see Kieval, *Languages of Community*, 110.

16. Anderson, *Kafka's Clothes*, 4. The "undying fire" is a quotation from a Kafka aphorism. See *BON*, 39.

17. *CS*, 222.

18. Ibid., 224.

19. Ibid., 225.

20. Ibid.

21. Ibid., 221–223.

22. Ibid., 223–225.

33. Ibid., 225.

24. Ibid., 222.

25. *T*, 83–90.

26. *CS*, 221.

27. Brod, *Franz Kafka*, 44.

28. *BON*, 87.

29. *T*, 228.

30. Ibid., 1.

31. *CS*, 89.

32. Ibid., 224.

33. *T*, 1.

34. Ibid., 3.

35. Ibid., 229.

36. *C*, 2.

37. Ibid., 46.

5. The Writer and His Worlds

1. *LF*, 288.

2. Ibid., 270.

3. Ibid., 279.

4. *D*, 104. I chose Ewald Oser's translation in Wagenbach, *Kafka*, 90, as far superior to the atrocious one by Joseph Kresch in the diaries.

5. *LF*, 22.

6. Ibid., 60.

7. *D*, 331.

8. Ibid., 333–334.

9. *LF*, 279.

10. Benno Wagner, "Kafka's Office Writings: Historical Background and Institutional Setting," in *Franz Kafka: The Office Writings*, ed. Stanley Corngold, Jack Greenberg, and Benno Wagner (Princeton, 2009), 42.

11. See Northey, *Kafka's Relatives*, 91.

12. *LFr*, 90.

13. Ibid., 92.

14. See in particular Scott Spector, *Prague Territories: National Conflict and Cultural Innovation in Franz Kafka's Fin de Siècle* (Berkeley, 2000), 16–17.

15. Brod, *Kafka*, 43–44.

16. Spector, *Prague Territories*, 17–18.

17. *LFr*, 205. For an interpretation of Ehrenfels's ideas and of *Cosmogony* specifically, see William M. Johnston, *The Austrian*

Mind: An Intellectual and Social History (Berkeley, 1983), 302–306, particularly 305–306.

18. Stanley Corngold, *Lambent Traces: Franz Kafka* (Princeton, 2004), xiii, xiv. For Sokel's thesis see mainly "Between Gnosticism and Jehovah: The Dilemma of Kafka's Religious Attitude" in Walter H. Sokel, *The Myth of Power and the Self: Essays on Franz Kafka* (Detroit, 2002), 292 ff. For the spread of Gnosticism in Prague, mainly under its Marcionist guise, see Johnston, *The Austrian Mind*, 270–273.

19. *D*, 46–47; also *TgbI*, 284–285.

20. Karen L. King, *What Is Gnosticism?* (Cambridge, MA, 2003), 45.

21. Max Brod, "Verzweiflung und Erlösung im Werk Franz Kafkas," in *Über Franz Kafka* (Frankfurt, 1974), 305.

22. Johnston, *The Austrian Mind*, 269–273.

23. Günther Anders, "Kafka pro und contra," in *Mensch ohne Welt* (Munich, 1993), 111–115.

24. For the exact quotation and reference see Hans-Gerd Koch, "Brods erlesener Kafka," in *Franz Kafka und die Weltliteratur*, ed. Manfred Engel and Dieter Lamping (Göttingen, 2006), 170n1. See also Brod, *Franz Kafka*, 61.

25. For these publication dates see Roger Hermes et al., *Franz Kafka: Eine Chronik* (Berlin, 1999), 50, 56.

26. *LFr*, 83.

27. *D*, 212–213.

28. Brod, *Kafka*, p 129.

29. *D*, 214.

30. Alt, *Franz Kafka*, 54.

31. *D*, 324.

32. Hermes et al., *Franz Kafka*, 145–146.

33. *D*, 302.

34. Quoted in Hermes et al., *Franz Kafka*, 45.

35. Stach, *Kafka: Die Jahre der Entscheidungen*, 463–465.

36. About Wolff's attitude, see Stach, *Kafka: Die Jahre der Erkenntnis*, 199–204.

37. For the publishing details see Joachim Unseld, *Franz*

Kafka: Ein Schriftstellerleben (Munich, 1982), and Joachim Unseld, "Kafkas Publikationen zu Lebzeiten," in *Kafka Handbuch*, ed. Bettina von Jagow and Oliver Jahraus (Göttingen, 2008), 123 ff.

38. Milan Kundera, *Les Testaments trahis* (Paris, 2000), 58.

39. Scott Spector, "Kafka und die literarische Moderne," in Jagow and Jahraus, *Kafka Handbuch*, 181 ff, particularly 191.

40. Anderson, *Kafka's Clothes*, 15.

41. Kafka "was no great reader—at least not in the sense of Thomas Mann, T. S. Eliot, Vladimir Nabokov or Jorge Luis Borges": Dieter Lamping, "Franz Kafka als Autor der Weltliteratur," in Engel and Lamping, *Franz Kafka und die Weltliteratur*, 9.

42. Hermes et al., *Franz Kafka*, 40.

43. About the influence of film technique on Kafka's narrative, particularly in *Amerika*, see Peter-André Alt, *Kafka und der Film: Über kinematographisches Erzählen* (Munich, 2009), 80 ff.

44. *LF*, 316.

45. See in particular Walter Hinderer, "'Kleist bläst in mich, wie eine alte Schweinsblase': Anmerkungen zu einer komplizierten Verwandschaft," in Engel and Lamping, *Franz Kafka und die Weltliteratur*, 66 ff.

46. *LF*, 157–158.

47. Jost Schillemeit, "Tolstoj Bezüge beim späten Kafka," in *Kafka-Studien*, ed. Rosemarie Schillemeit (Göttingen, 2004), 164 ff.

48. *D*, 230.

49. Quoted in Joakim Garff, *Søren Kierkegaard: A Biography* (Princeton, 2005), 250.

50. Ibid.

51. Ibid., 261. Farinelli (Carlo Broschi), an eighteenth-century opera singer, considered one of the greatest ever, was castrated in his childhood to preserve his voice.

52. *LFr*, 162.

53. Ibid., 171.

54. Ibid., 190.

55. Ibid., 195.

56. Ibid., 199.

57. Søren Kierkegaard, *Either/Or: A Fragment of Life* (London, 2004), 105.

58. *LFr*, 202–203.

59. *BON*, 29.

60. *D*, 301.

61. Ibid., 204.

62. Ibid., 302.

63. Ibid.

64. Hans-Gerd Koch, "Brod's erlesener Kafka," in Engel and Lamping, *Franz Kafka und die Weltliteratur*, 177. For one of the most recent attempts to prove Kafka's social and political involvement see Pascale Casanova, *Kafka en colère* (Paris, 2011).

65. In 1910, Kafka read Michail Kusmin's biography of Alexander the Great; *D*, 32.

66. *D*, 115.

67. Ibid.

68. Ibid., 344–348.

69. Ibid., 80 (the translation has been reworked).

70. Ibid., 81.

71. *LFr*, 273–274.

72. *D*, 336 (translation slightly altered).

73. Ibid., 389–390.

74. *LFr*, 285.

75. *BON*, 52.

6. An Ultimate Quest for Meaning?

1. *D*, 406–407.

2. *LFr*, 333 ff.

3. Ibid., 332.

4. Ibid.

5. *TgbIII*, 233.

6. About the initial first-person writing of *The Castle* see Michael Müller, "Das Schloss," in Jagow and Jahraus, *Kafka Handbuch*, 528n2.

7. *D*, 404.

8. Ibid., 402.

9. *T*, 228.

10. *D*, 395.

11. Ibid., 398.

12. Ibid.

13. Ibid., 410.

14. *D*, 400.

15. *TgbIII*, 199.

16. *LFr*, 373.

17. Ibid., 405.

18. Ibid., 411.

19. Ibid., 412.

20. *LFr*, 417.

21. Hermes et al., *Franz Kafka*, 205.

22. Nicolas Murray, *Kafka* (London, 2004), 385. For some details about the memorial service see Brod, *Streitbares Leben*, 192.

23. *C*, 106.

24. *BON*, 30.

25. Eric L. Santner, *On Creaturely Life: Rilke, Benjamin, Sebald* (Chicago, 2006), 22.

26. Franz Kafka, *Amerika: The Man Who Disappeared*, trans. Michael Hofmann (New York, 2004), 218.

27. *BON*, 29.

28. Ibid.

29. Max Brod, "Franz Kafkas Glauben und Lehre," in *Über Franz Kafka*, 223.

30. *T*, 216.

31. Ibid., 220.

32. *D*, 423.

33. *CS*, 327.

34. Ibid., 325.

35. Ibid., 276.

36. Ibid., 361.

INDEX OF NAMES

JEWISH LIVES is a major series of interpretive
biography designed to illuminate the imprint of Jewish
figures upon literature, religion, philosophy, politics, cultural and
economic life, and the arts and sciences. Subjects are paired with
authors to elicit lively, deeply informed books that explore the
range and depth of Jewish experience
from antiquity through the present.

Jewish Lives is a partnership of Yale University Press
and the Leon D. Black Foundation.

Ileene Smith is editorial director. Anita Shapira and
Steven J. Zipperstein are series editors.

Library of Congress Cataloging-in-Publication Data

Friedländer, Saul, 1932-. Franz Kafka : the poet of shame and guilt / Saul Friedländer.
    p.   cm. — (Jewish lives)
Includes bibliographical references and index.
ISBN 978-0-300-13661-6 (cloth : alk. paper) 1. Kafka, Franz, 1883-1924. 2. Authors,
Austrian — 20th century — Biography. 3. Jewish authors — Austria — Biography. I. Title.
PT2621.A26Z7199265 2013
833'.912 — dc23
[B]

                                                                        2012034381

Yale University Press books may be purchased in quantity for educational, business,
or promotional use. For information, please e-mail sales.press@yale.edu (U.S. office)
or sales@yaleup.co.uk (U.K. office).

Set in Janson Oldstyle type by Tseng Information Systems, Inc.

Printed in the United States of America.

A catalogue record for this book is available from the British Library.

This paper meets the requirements of ANSI/NISO Z39.48-1992 (Permanence of Paper).